Apache Mahout Essentials

Implement top-notch machine learning algorithms
for classification, clustering, and recommendations
with Apache Mahout

Jayani Withanawasam

BIRMINGHAM - MUMBAI

Apache Mahout Essentials

First published: June 2015

Production reference: 1120615

Published by Packt Publishing Ltd.
Livery Place
35 Livery Street
Birmingham B3 2PB, UK.

ISBN 978-1-78355-499-7

www.packtpub.com

Credits

Author
Jayani Withanawasam

Reviewers
Guillaume Agis

Saleem A. Ansari

Sahil Kharb

Pavan Kumar Narayanan

Commissioning Editor
Akram Hussain

Acquisition Editor
Shaon Basu

Content Development Editor
Nikhil Potdukhe

Technical Editor
Tanmayee Patil

Copy Editor
Dipti Kapadia

Project Coordinator
Vijay Kushlani

Proofreader
Safis Editing

Indexer
Tejal Soni

Graphics
Sheetal Aute

Jason Monteiro

Production Coordinator
Melwyn D'sa

Cover Work
Melwyn D'sa

About the Author

Jayani Withanawasam is R&D engineer and a senior software engineer at Zaizi Asia, where she focuses on applying machine learning techniques to provide smart content management solutions.

She is currently pursuing an MSc degree in artificial intelligence at the University of Moratuwa, Sri Lanka, and has completed her BE in software engineering (with first class honors) from the University of Westminster, UK.

She has more than 6 years of industry experience, and she has worked in areas such as machine learning, natural language processing, and semantic web technologies during her tenure.

She is passionate about working with semantic technologies and big data.

First of all, I would like to thank the Apache Mahout contributors for the invaluable effort that they have put in the project, crafting it as a popular scalable machine learning library in the industry.

Also, I would like to thank Rafa Haro for leading me toward the exciting world of machine learning and natural language processing.

I am sincerely grateful to Shaon Basu, an acquisition editor at Packt Publishing, and Nikhil Potdukhe, a content development editor at Packt Publishing, for their remarkable guidance and encouragement as I wrote this book amid my other commitments.

Furthermore, my heartfelt gratitude goes to Abinia Sachithanantham and Dedunu Dhananjaya for motivating me throughout the journey of writing the book.

Last but not least, I am eternally thankful to my parents for staying by my side throughout all my pursuits and being pillars of strength.

About the Reviewers

Guillaume Agis is a French 25 year old with a master's degree in computer science from Epitech, where he studied for 4 years in France and 1 year in Finland.

Open-minded and interested in a lot of domains, such as healthcare, innovation, high-tech, and science, he is always open to new adventures and experiments. Currently, he works as a software engineer in London at a company called Touch Surgery, where he is developing an application. The application is a surgery simulator that allows you to practice and rehearse operations even before setting foot in the operating room.

His previous jobs were, for the most part, in R&D, where he worked with very innovative technologies, such as Mahout, to implement collaborative filtering into artificial intelligence.

He always does his best to bring his team to the top and tries to make a difference.

He's also helping while42, a worldwide alumni network of French engineers, to grow as well as manage the London chapter.

I would like to thank all the people who have brought me to the top and helped me become what I am now.

Saleem A. Ansari is a full stack Java/Scala/Ruby developer with over 7 years of industry experience and a special interest in machine learning and information retrieval. Having implemented data ingestion and processing pipeline in Core Java and Ruby separately, he knows the challenges faced by huge datasets in such systems. He has worked for companies such as Red Hat, Impetus Technologies, Belzabar Software Design, and Exzeo Software Pvt Ltd. He is also a passionate member of the Free and Open Source Software (FOSS) Community. He started his journey with FOSS in the year 2004. In 2005, he formed JMILUG - Linux User's Group at Jamia Millia Islamia University, New Delhi. Since then, he has been contributing to FOSS by organizing community activities and also by contributing code to various projects (`http://github.com/tuxdna`). He also mentors students on FOSS and its benefits. He is currently enrolled at Georgia Institute of Technology, USA, on the MSCS program. He can be reached at `tuxdna@fedoraproject.org`.

Apart from reviewing this book, he maintains a blog at `http://tuxdna.in/`.

First of all, I would like to thank the vibrant, talented, and generous Apache Mahout community that created such a wonderful machine learning library. I would like to thank Packt Publishing and its staff for giving me this wonderful opportunity. I would like to thank the author for his hard work in simplifying and elaborating on the latest information in Apache Mahout.

Sahil Kharb has recently graduated from the Indian Institute of Technology, Jodhpur (India), and is working at Rockon Technologies. In the past, he has worked on Mahout and Hadoop for the last two years. His area of interest is data mining on a large scale. Nowadays, he works on Apache Spark and Apache Storm, doing real-time data analytics and batch processing with the help of Apache Mahout.

He has also reviewed *Learning Apache Mahout, Packt Publishing*.

I would like to thank my family, for their unconditional love and support, and God Almighty, for giving me strength and endurance. Also, I am thankful to my friend Chandni, who helped me in testing the code.

Pavan Kumar Narayanan is an applied mathematician with over 3 years of experience in mathematical programming, data science, and analytics. Currently based in New York, he has worked to build a marketing analytics product for a startup using Apache Mahout and has published and presented papers in algorithmic research at Transportation Research Board, Washington DC, and SUNY Research Conference, Albany, New York. He also runs a blog, DataScience Hacks (https://datasciencehacks.wordpress.com/). His interests are exploring new problem solving techniques and software, from industrial mathematics to machine learning writing book reviews.

Pavan can be contacted at pavan.narayanan@gmail.com.

I would like to thank my family, for their unconditional love and support, and God Almighty, for giving me strength and endurance.

www.PacktPub.com

Support files, eBooks, discount offers, and more

For support files and downloads related to your book, please visit www.PacktPub.com.

Did you know that Packt offers eBook versions of every book published, with PDF and ePub files available? You can upgrade to the eBook version at www.PacktPub.com and as a print book customer, you are entitled to a discount on the eBook copy. Get in touch with us at service@packtpub.com for more details.

At www.PacktPub.com, you can also read a collection of free technical articles, sign up for a range of free newsletters and receive exclusive discounts and offers on Packt books and eBooks.

https://www2.packtpub.com/books/subscription/packtlib

Do you need instant solutions to your IT questions? PacktLib is Packt's online digital book library. Here, you can search, access, and read Packt's entire library of books.

Why subscribe?

- Fully searchable across every book published by Packt
- Copy and paste, print, and bookmark content
- On demand and accessible via a web browser

Free access for Packt account holders

If you have an account with Packt at www.PacktPub.com, you can use this to access PacktLib today and view 9 entirely free books. Simply use your login credentials for immediate access.

Table of Contents

Preface

Apache Mahout is a scalable machine learning library that provides algorithms for classification, clustering, and recommendations.

This book helps you to use Apache Mahout to implement widely used machine learning algorithms in order to gain better insights about large and complex datasets in a scalable manner.

Starting from fundamental concepts in machine learning and Apache Mahout, real-world applications, a diverse range of popular algorithms and their implementations, code examples, evaluation strategies, and best practices are given for each machine learning technique. Further, this book contains a complete step-by-step guide to set up Apache Mahout in the production environment, using Apache Hadoop to unleash the scalable power of Apache Mahout in a distributed environment. Finally, you are guided toward the data visualization techniques for Apache Mahout, which make your data come alive!

What this book covers

Chapter 1, *Introducing Apache Mahout*, provides an introduction to machine learning and Apache Mahout.

Chapter 2, *Clustering*, provides an introduction to unsupervised learning and clustering techniques (K-Means clustering and other algorithms) in Apache Mahout along with performance optimization tips for clustering.

Chapter 3, *Regression and Classification*, provides an introduction to supervised learning and classification techniques (linear regression, logistic regression, Naïve Bayes, and HMMs) in Apache Mahout.

Chapter 4, Recommendations, provides a comparison between collaborative- and content-based filtering and recommenders in Apache Mahout (user-based, item-based, and matrix-factorization-based).

Chapter 5, Apache Mahout in Production, provides a guide to scaling Apache Mahout in the production environment with Apache Hadoop.

Chapter 6, Visualization, provides a guide to visualizing data using D3.js.

What you need for this book

The following software libraries are needed at various phases of this book:

*   Java 1.7 or above
*   Apache Mahout
*   Apache Hadoop
*   Apache Spark
*   D3.js

Who this book is for

If you are a Java developer or a data scientist who has not worked with Apache Mahout previously and want to get up to speed on implementing machine learning on big data, then this is a concise and fast-paced guide for you.

Conventions

In this book, you will find a number of text styles that distinguish between different kinds of information. Here are some examples of these styles and an explanation of their meaning.

Code words in text, database table names, folder names, filenames, file extensions, pathnames, dummy URLs, user input, and Twitter handles are shown as follows: "Save the following content in a file named as KmeansTest.data."

A block of code is set as follows:

```
<dependency>
    <groupId>org.apache.mahout</groupId>
    <artifactId>mahout-core</artifactId>
    <version>${mahout.version}</version>
</dependency>
```

When we wish to draw your attention to a particular part of a code block, the relevant lines or items are set in bold:

```
private static final String DIRECTORY_CONTAINING_CONVERTED_INPUT =
"Kmeansdata";
```

Any command-line input or output is written as follows:

```
mahout seq2sparse -i kmeans/sequencefiles -o kmeans/sparse
```

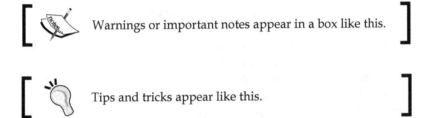

Warnings or important notes appear in a box like this.

Tips and tricks appear like this.

Reader feedback

Feedback from our readers is always welcome. Let us know what you think about this book—what you liked or disliked. Reader feedback is important for us as it helps us develop titles that you will really get the most out of.

To send us general feedback, simply e-mail feedback@packtpub.com, and mention the book's title in the subject of your message.

If there is a topic that you have expertise in and you are interested in either writing or contributing to a book, see our author guide at www.packtpub.com/authors.

Customer support

Now that you are the proud owner of a Packt book, we have a number of things to help you to get the most from your purchase.

Downloading the example code

You can download the example code files from your account at http://www.packtpub.com for all the Packt Publishing books you have purchased. If you purchased this book elsewhere, you can visit http://www.packtpub.com/support and register to have the files e-mailed directly to you.

Downloading the color images of this book

We also provide you with a PDF file that has color images of the screenshots/ diagrams used in this book. The color images will help you better understand the changes in the output. You can download this file from `https://www.packtpub.com/sites/default/files/downloads/B03506_4997OS_Graphics.pdf`.

Errata

Although we have taken every care to ensure the accuracy of our content, mistakes do happen. If you find a mistake in one of our books—maybe a mistake in the text or the code—we would be grateful if you could report this to us. By doing so, you can save other readers from frustration and help us improve subsequent versions of this book. If you find any errata, please report them by visiting `http://www.packtpub.com/submit-errata`, selecting your book, clicking on the **Errata Submission Form** link, and entering the details of your errata. Once your errata are verified, your submission will be accepted and the errata will be uploaded to our website or added to any list of existing errata under the Errata section of that title.

To view the previously submitted errata, go to `https://www.packtpub.com/books/content/support` and enter the name of the book in the search field. The required information will appear under the **Errata** section.

Piracy

Piracy of copyrighted material on the Internet is an ongoing problem across all media. At Packt, we take the protection of our copyright and licenses very seriously. If you come across any illegal copies of our works in any form on the Internet, please provide us with the location address or website name immediately so that we can pursue a remedy.

Please contact us at `copyright@packtpub.com` with a link to the suspected pirated material.

We appreciate your help in protecting our authors and our ability to bring you valuable content.

Questions

If you have a problem with any aspect of this book, you can contact us at `questions@packtpub.com`, and we will do our best to address the problem.

1
Introducing Apache Mahout

As you may be already aware, Apache Mahout is an open source library
of scalable machine learning algorithms that focuses on clustering, classification,
and recommendations.

This chapter will provide an introduction to machine learning and Apache Mahout.

In this chapter, we will cover the following topics:

- Machine learning in a nutshell
- Machine learning applications
- Machine learning libraries
- The history of machine learning
- Apache Mahout
- Setting up Apache Mahout
- How Apache Mahout works
- From Hadoop MapReduce to Spark
- When is it appropriate to use Apache Mahout?

Machine learning in a nutshell

*"Machine learning is the most exciting field of all the computer sciences.
Sometimes I actually think that machine learning is not only the most exciting
thing in computer science, but also the most exciting thing in all of human
endeavor."*

– Andrew Ng, Associate Professor at Stanford and Chief Scientist of Baidu

Giving a detailed explanation of machine learning is beyond the scope of this book. For this purpose, there are other excellent resources that I have listed here:

- *Machine Learning* by Andrew Ng at Coursera (`https://www.coursera.org/course/ml`)
- *Foundations of Machine Learning (Adaptive Computation and Machine Learning series)* by Mehryar Mohri, Afshin Rostamizadeh, and Ameet Talwalker

However, basic machine learning concepts are explained very briefly here, for those who are not familiar with it.

Machine learning is an area of artificial intelligence that focuses on learning from the available data to make predictions on unseen data without explicit programming.

To solve real-world problems using machine learning, we first need to represent the characteristics of the problem domain using features.

Features

A feature is a distinct, measurable, heuristic property of the item of interest being perceived. We need to consider the features that have the greatest potential in discriminating between different categories.

Supervised learning versus unsupervised learning

Let's explain the difference between supervised learning and unsupervised learning using a simple example of pebbles:

- **Supervised learning**: Take a collection of mixed pebbles, as given in the preceding figure, and categorize (label) them as small, medium, and large pebbles. Examples of supervised learning are regression and classification.

- **Unsupervised learning**: Here, just group them based on similar sizes but don't label them. An example of unsupervised learning is clustering.

For a machine to perform learning tasks, it requires features such as the diameter and weight of each pebble.

This book will cover how to implement the following machine learning techniques using Apache Mahout:

- Clustering
- Classification and regression
- Recommendations

Machine learning applications

Do you know that machine learning has a significant impact in real-life day-to-day applications? World's popular organizations, such as Google, Facebook, Yahoo!, and Amazon, use machine learning algorithms in their applications.

Information retrieval

Information retrieval is an area where machine learning is vastly applied in the industry. Some examples include Google News, Google target advertisements, and Amazon product recommendations.

Google News uses machine learning to categorize large volumes of online news articlesL:

The relevance of Google target advertisements can be improved by using machine learning:

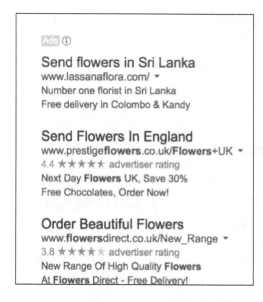

Amazon as well as most of the e-business websites use machine learning to understand which products will interest the users:

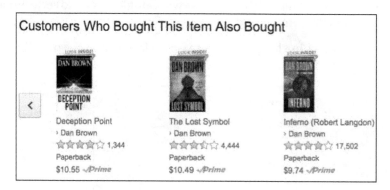

Even though information retrieval is the area that has commercialized most of the machine learning applications, machine learning can be applied in various other areas, such as business and health care.

Business

Machine learning is applied to solve different business problems, such as market segmentation, business analytics, risk classification, and stock market predictions.

A few of them are explained here.

Market segmentation (clustering)

In market segmentation, clustering techniques can be used to identify the homogeneous subsets of consumers, as shown in the following figure:

Take an example of a **Fast-Moving Consumer Goods** (**FMCG**) company that introduces a shampoo for personal use. They can use clustering to identify the different market segments, by considering features such as the number of people who have hair fall, colored hair, dry hair, and normal hair. Then, they can decide on the types of shampoo required for different market segments, which will maximize the profit.

Stock market predictions (regression)

Regression techniques can be used to predict future trends in stocks by considering features such as closing prices and foreign currency rates.

Health care

Machine learning is heavily used in medical image processing in the health care sector. Using a mammogram for cancer tissue detection is one example of this.

Using a mammogram for cancer tissue detection

Classification techniques can be used for the early detection of breast cancers by analyzing the mammograms with image processing, as shown in the following figure, which is a difficult task for humans due to irregular pathological structures and noise.

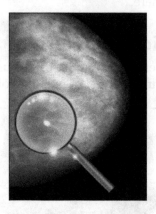

Machine learning libraries

Machine learning libraries can be categorized using different criteria, which are explained in the sections that follow.

Open source or commercial

Free and open source libraries are cost-effective solutions, and most of them provide a framework that allows you to implement new algorithms on your own. However, support for these libraries is not as good as the support available for proprietary libraries. However, some open source libraries have very active mailing lists to address this issue.

Apache Mahout, OpenCV, MLib, and Mallet are some open source libraries.

MATLAB is a commercial numerical environment that contains a machine learning library.

Scalability

Machine learning algorithms are resource-intensive (CPU, memory, and storage) operations. Also, most of the time, they are applied on large volumes of datasets. So, decentralization (for example, data and algorithms), distribution, and replication techniques are used to scale out a system:

- Apache Mahout (data distributed over clusters and parallel algorithms)
- Spark MLib (distributed memory-based Spark architecture)
- MLPACK (low memory or CPU requirements due to the use of C++)
- GraphLab (multicore parallelism)

Languages used

Most of the machine learning libraries are implemented using languages such as Java, C#, C++, Python, and Scala.

Algorithm support

Machine learning libraries, such as R and Weka, have many machine learning algorithms implemented. However, they are not scalable. So, when it comes to scalable machine learning libraries, Apache Mahout has better algorithm support than Spark MLib at the moment, as Spark MLib is relatively young.

Batch processing versus stream processing

Stream processing mechanisms, for example, Jubatus and Samoa, update a model instantaneously just after receiving data using incremental learning.

In batch processing, data is collected over a period of time and then processed together. In the context of machine learning, the model is updated after collecting data for a period of time. The batch processing mechanism (for example, Apache Mahout) is mostly suitable for processing large volumes of data.

LIBSVM implements support vector machines and it is specialized for that purpose.

A comparison of some of the popular machine learning libraries is given in the following table *Table 1: Comparison between popular machine learning libraries*:

Machine learning library	Open source or commercial	Scalable?	Language used	Algorithm support
MATLAB	Commercial	No	Mostly C	High
R packages	Open source	No	R	High
Weka	Open source	No	Java	High
Sci-Kit Learn	Open source	No	Python	
Apache Mahout	Open source	Yes	Java	Medium
Spark MLib	Open source	Yes	Scala	Low
Samoa	Open source	Yes	Java	

The story so far

The following timeline will give you an idea about the way machine learning has evolved and the maturity of the available machine learning libraries. Also, it is evident that even though machine learning was found in 1952, popular machine learning libraries have begun to evolve very recently.

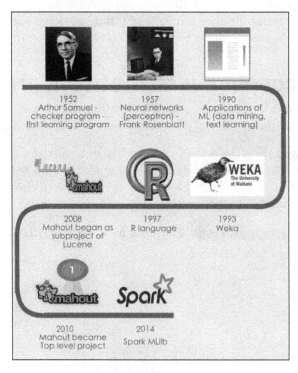

Apache Mahout

In this section, we will have a quick look at Apache Mahout.

Do you know how Mahout got its name?

As you can see in the logo, a **mahout** is a person who drives an elephant. Hadoop's logo is an elephant. So, this is an indicator that Mahout's goal is to use Hadoop in the right manner.

The following are the features of Mahout:

- It is a project of the Apache software foundation
- It is a scalable machine learning library
    - The MapReduce implementation scales linearly with the data
    - Fast sequential algorithms (the runtime does not depend on the size of the dataset)
- It mainly contains clustering, classification, and recommendation (collaborative filtering) algorithms
- Here, machine learning algorithms can be executed in sequential (in-memory mode) or distributed mode (MapReduce is enabled)
- Most of the algorithms are implemented using the MapReduce paradigm
- It runs on top of the Hadoop framework for scaling
- Data is stored in HDFS (data storage) or in memory
- It is a Java library (no user interface!)
- The latest released version is 0.9, and 1.0 is coming soon
- It is not a domain-specific but a general purpose library

For those of you who are curious! What are the problems that Mahout is trying to solve? The following problems that Mahout is trying to solve:

The amount of available data is growing drastically.

The computer hardware market is geared toward providing better performance in computers. Machine learning algorithms are computationally expensive algorithms. However, there was no framework sufficient to harness the power of hardware (multicore computers) to gain better performance.

The need for a parallel programming framework to speed up machine learning algorithms.

Mahout is a general parallelization for machine learning algorithms (the parallelization method is not algorithm-specific).

No specialized optimizations are required to improve the performance of each algorithm; you just need to add some more cores.

Linear speed up with number of cores.

Each algorithm, such as Naïve Bayes, K-Means, and Expectation-maximization, is expressed in the summation form. (I will explain this in detail in future chapters.)

For more information, please read *Map-Reduce for Machine Learning on Multicore*, which can be found at http://www.cs.stanford.edu/people/ang/papers/nips06-mapreducemulticore.pdf.

Setting up Apache Mahout

Download the latest release of Mahout from https://mahout.apache.org/general/downloads.html.

If you are referencing Mahout as a Maven project, add the following dependency in the pom.xml file:

```
<dependency>
    <groupId>org.apache.mahout</groupId>
    <artifactId>mahout-core</artifactId>
    <version>${mahout.version}</version>
</dependency>
```

If required, add the following Maven dependencies as well:

```
<dependency>
  <groupId>org.apache.mahout</groupId>
  <artifactId>mahout-math</artifactId>
  <version>${mahout.version}</version>
</dependency>
<dependency>
  <groupId>org.apache.mahout</groupId>
  <artifactId>mahout-integration</artifactId>
  <version>${mahout.version}</version>
</dependency>
```

> **Downloading the example code**
>
> You can download the example code files from your account at http://www.packtpub.com for all the Packt Publishing books you have purchased. If you purchased this book elsewhere, you can visit http://www.packtpub.com/support and register to have the files e-mailed directly to you.

More details on setting up a Maven project can be found at http://maven.apache.org/.

Follow the instructions given at https://mahout.apache.org/developers/buildingmahout.html to build Mahout from the source.

The Mahout command-line launcher is located at bin/mahout.

How Apache Mahout works?

Let's take a look at the various components of Mahout.

The high-level design

The following table represents the high-level design of a Mahout implementation. Machine learning applications access the API, which provides support for implementing different machine learning techniques, such as clustering, classification, and recommendations.

Also, if the application requires preprocessing (for example, stop word removal and stemming) for text input, it can be achieved with Apache Lucene. Apache Hadoop provides data processing and storage to enable scalable processing.

Also, there will be performance optimizations using Java Collections and the Mahout-Math library. The Mahout-integration library contains utilities such as displaying the data and results.

Machine Learning Applications			
Clustering	Classification	Recommendations	
Mahout-math			Text Preprocessing (Apache Lucene)
Mahout-integration	Java collections	Apache Hadoop	
Mahout-core			

The distribution

MapReduce is a programming paradigm to enable parallel processing. When it is applied to machine learning, we assign one MapReduce engine to one algorithm (for each MapReduce engine, one master is assigned).

Input is provided as Hadoop sequence files, which consist of binary key-value pairs. The master node manages the mappers and reducers. Once the input is represented as sequence files and sent to the master, it splits data and assigns the data to different mappers, which are other nodes. Then, it collects the intermediate outcome from mappers and sends them to related reducers for further processing. Lastly, the final outcome is generated.

From Hadoop MapReduce to Spark

Let's take a look at the journey from MapReduce to Spark.

Problems with Hadoop MapReduce

Even though MapReduce provides a suitable programming model for batch data processing, it does not perform well with real-time data processing. When it comes to iterative machine learning algorithms, it is necessary to carry information across iterations. Moreover, an intermediate outcome needs to be persisted during each iteration. Therefore, it is necessary to store and retrieve temporary data from the **Hadoop Distributed File System (HDFS)** very frequently, which incurs significant performance degradation.

Machine learning algorithms that can be written in a certain form of summation (algorithms that fit in the statistical query model) can be implemented in the MapReduce programming model. However, some of the machine learning algorithms are hard to implement by adhering to the MapReduce programming paradigm. MapReduce cannot be applied if there are any computational dependencies between the data.

Therefore, this constrained programming model is a barrier for Apache Mahout as it can limit the number of supported distributed algorithms.

In-memory data processing with Spark and H2O

Apache Spark is a large-scale scalable data processing framework, which claims to be 100 times faster than Hadoop MapReduce when in memory and 10 times faster in disk, has a distributed memory-based architecture. H2O is an open source, parallel processing engine for machine learning by 0xdata.

As a solution to the problems of the Hadoop MapReduce approach mentioned previously, Apache Mahout is working on integrating Apache Spark and H2O as the backend integration (with the Mahout Math library).

Why is Mahout shifting from Hadoop MapReduce to Spark?

With Spark, there can be better support for iterative machine learning algorithms using the in-memory approach. In-memory applications are self-optimizing. An algebraic expression optimizer is used for distributed linear algebra. One significant example is the **Distributed Row Matrix** (**DRM**), which is a huge matrix partitioned by rows.

Further, programming with Spark is easier than programming with MapReduce because Spark decouples the machine learning logic from the distributed backend. Accordingly, the distribution is hidden from the machine learning API users. This can be used like R or MATLAB.

When is it appropriate to use Apache Mahout?

You should consider the following aspects before making a decision to use Apache Mahout as your machine learning library:

- Are you looking for a machine learning algorithm for industry use with performance as a critical evaluation factor?
- Are you looking for a free and open source solution?
- Is your dataset large and growing at an alarming rate? (MATLAB, Weka, Octave, and R can be used to process KBs and MBs of data, but if your data volume is growing up to the GB level, then it is better to use Mahout.)
- Do you want batch data processing as opposed to real-time data processing?
- Are you looking for a mature library, which has been there in the market for a few years?

If all or most of the preceding considerations are met, then Mahout is the right solution for you.

Summary

Machine learning is about discovering hidden insights or patterns from the available data. Machine learning algorithms can be divided in two categories: supervised learning and unsupervised learning. There are many real-world applications of machine learning in diverse domains, such as information retrieval, business, and health care.

Apache Mahout is a scalable machine learning library that runs on top of the Hadoop framework. In v0.10, Apache Mahout is shifting toward Apache Spark and H20 to address performance and usability issues that occur due to the MapReduce programming paradigm.

In the upcoming chapters, we will dive deep into different machine learning techniques.

2
Clustering

This chapter explains the clustering technique in machine learning and its implementation using Apache Mahout.

The K-Means clustering algorithm is explained in detail with both Java and command-line examples (sequential and parallel executions), and other important clustering algorithms, such as Fuzzy K-Means, canopy clustering, and spectral K-Means are also explored.

In this chapter, we will cover the following topics:

- Unsupervised learning and clustering
- Applications of clustering
- Types of clustering
- K-Means clustering
- K-Means clustering with MapReduce
- Other clustering algorithms
- Text clustering
- Optimizing clustering performance

Unsupervised learning and clustering

Information is a key driver for any type of organization. However, with the rapid growth in the volume of data, valuable information may be hidden and go unnoticed due to the lack of effective data processing and analyzing mechanisms.

Clustering is an unsupervised learning mechanism that can find the hidden patterns and structures in data by finding data points that are similar to each other. No prelabeling is required. So, you can organize data using clustering with little or no human intervention.

For example, let's say you are given a collection of balls of different sizes without any category labels, such as big and small, attached to them; you should be able to categorize them using clustering by considering their attributes, such as radius and weight, for similarity.

In this chapter, you will learn how to use Apache Mahout to perform clustering using different algorithms.

Applications of clustering

Clustering has many applications in different domains, such as biology, business, and information retrieval. A few of them are shown in the following image:

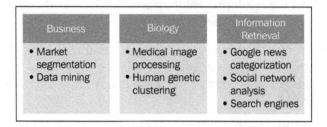

Computer vision and image processing

Clustering techniques are widely used in the computer vision and image processing domain. Clustering is used for image segmentation in medical image processing for **computer aided disease** (**CAD**) diagnosis. One specific area is breast cancer detection.

In breast cancer detection, a mammogram is clustered into several parts for further analysis, as shown in the following image. The regions of interest for signs of breast cancer in the mammogram can be identified using the K-Means algorithm, which is explained later in this chapter.

Image features such as pixels, colors, intensity, and texture are used during clustering:

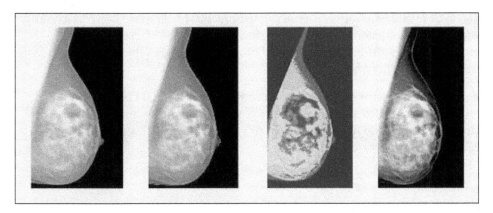

Types of clustering

Clustering can be divided into different categories based on different criteria.

Hard clustering versus soft clustering

Clustering techniques can be divided into hard clustering and soft clustering based on the cluster's membership.

In hard clustering, a given data point in n-dimensional space only belongs to one cluster. This is also known as exclusive clustering. The K-Means clustering mechanism is an example of hard clustering.

A given data point can belong to more than one cluster in soft clustering. This is also known as overlapping clustering. The Fuzzy K-Means algorithm is a good example of soft clustering. A visual representation of the difference between hard clustering and soft clustering is given in the following figure:

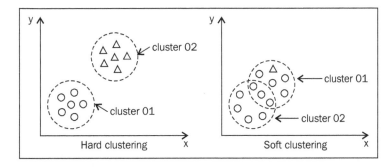

Flat clustering versus hierarchical clustering

In hierarchical clustering, a hierarchy of clusters is built using the top-down (divisive) or bottom-up (agglomerative) approach. This is more informative and accurate than flat clustering, which is a simple technique where no hierarchy is present. However, this comes at the cost of performance, as flat clustering is faster and more efficient than hierarchical clustering.

For example, let's assume that you need to figure out T-shirt sizes for people of different sizes. Using hierarchal clustering, you can come up with sizes for small (s), medium (m), and large (l) first by analyzing a sample of the people in the population. Then, we can further categorize this as extra small (xs), small (s), medium, large (l), and extra large (xl) sizes.

Model-based clustering

In model-based clustering, data is modeled using a standard statistical model to work with different distributions. The idea is to find a model that best fits the data. The best-fit model is achieved by tuning up parameters to minimize loss on errors. Once the parameter values are set, probability membership can be calculated for new data points using the model. Model-based clustering gives a probability distribution over clusters.

K-Means clustering

K-Means clustering is a simple and fast clustering algorithm that has been widely adopted in many problem domains. In this chapter, we will give a detailed explanation of the K-Means algorithm, as it will provide the base for other algorithms. K-Means clustering assigns data points to *k* number of clusters (cluster centroids) by minimizing the distance from the data points to the cluster centroids.

Let's consider a simple scenario where we need to cluster people based on their size (height and weight are the selected attributes) and different colors (clusters):

We can plot this problem in two-dimensional space, as shown in the following figure and solve it using the K-Means algorithm:

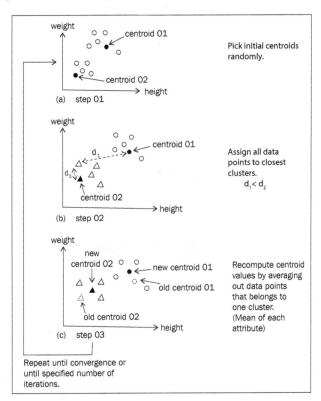

Getting your hands dirty!

Let's move on to a real implementation of the K-Means algorithm using Apache Mahout. The following are the different ways in which you can run algorithms in Apache Mahout:

- Sequential
- MapReduce

You can execute the algorithms using a command line (by calling the correct `bin/mahout` subcommand) or using Java programming (calling the correct driver's `run` method).

Running K-Means using Java programming

This example continues with the people-clustering scenario mentioned earlier.

The size (weight and height) distribution for this example has been plotted in two-dimensional space, as shown in the following image:

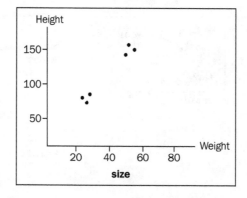

Data preparation

First, we need to represent the problem domain as numerical vectors.

The following table shows the size distribution of people mentioned in the previous scenario:

Weight (kg)	Height (cm)
22	80
25	75
28	85
55	150
50	145
53	153

Save the following content in a file named `KmeansTest.data`:

```
22 80
25 75
28 85
55 150
50 145
53 153
```

Understanding important parameters

Let's take a look at the significance of some important parameters:

- `org.apache.hadoop.fs.Path`: This denotes the path to a file or directory in the filesystem.
- `org.apache.hadoop.conf.Configuration`: This provides access to Hadoop-related configuration parameters.
- `org.apache.mahout.common.distance.DistanceMeasure`: This determines the distance between two points. Different distance measures are given and explained later in this chapter.
- `K`: This denotes the number of clusters.
- `convergenceDelta`: This is a double value that is used to determine whether the algorithm has converged.
- `maxIterations`: This denotes the maximum number of iterations to run.
- `runClustering`: If this is `true`, the clustering step is to be executed after the clusters have been determined.
- `runSequential`: If this is `true`, the K-Means sequential implementation is to be used in order to process the input data.

The following code snippet shows the source code:

```
private static final String DIRECTORY_CONTAINING_CONVERTED_INPUT =
"Kmeansdata";

public static void main(String[] args) throws Exception {

  // Path to output folder
  Path output = new Path("Kmeansoutput");

  // Hadoop configuration details
  Configuration conf = new Configuration();
  HadoopUtil.delete(conf, output);

  run(conf, new Path("KmeansTest"), output, new
  EuclideanDistanceMeasure(), 2, 0.5, 10);
}

public static void run(Configuration conf, Path input, Path
output, DistanceMeasure measure, int k,
double convergenceDelta, int maxIterations) throws Exception {

  // Input should be given as sequence file format
  Path directoryContainingConvertedInput = new Path(output,
  DIRECTORY_CONTAINING_CONVERTED_INPUT);
  InputDriver.runJob(input, directoryContainingConvertedInput,
  "org.apache.mahout.math.RandomAccessSparseVector");

  // Get initial clusters randomly
  Path clusters = new Path(output, "random-seeds");
  clusters = RandomSeedGenerator.buildRandom(conf,
  directoryContainingConvertedInput, clusters, k, measure);

  // Run K-Means with a given K
  KMeansDriver.run(conf, directoryContainingConvertedInput,
clusters, output, convergenceDelta,
  maxIterations, true, 0.0, false);

  // run ClusterDumper to display result
  Path outGlob = new Path(output, "clusters-*-final");
  Path clusteredPoints = new Path(output,"clusteredPoints");

  ClusterDumper clusterDumper = new ClusterDumper(outGlob,
  clusteredPoints);
  clusterDumper.printClusters(null);
}
```

The console output is shown in the following image. The details of the two clusters that are formed, positions of the centroids, and distance from centroids to each data point are given in this output:

```
VL-5{n=3 c=[52.667, 149.333] r=[2.055, 3.300]}
      Weight : [props - optional]:  Point:
      1.0 : [distance=2.4267032964268394]: 2 = [55.000, 150.000]
      1.0 : [distance=5.088112507491256]: 2 = [50.000, 145.000]
      1.0 : [distance=3.6817870057290776]: 2 = [53.000, 153.000]
VL-1{n=3 c=[25.000, 80.000] r=[2.449, 4.082]}
      Weight : [props - optional]:  Point:
      1.0 : [distance=3.0]: 2 = [22.000, 80.000]
      1.0 : [distance=5.0]: 2 = [25.000, 75.000]
      1.0 : [distance=5.830951894845301]: 2 = [28.000, 85.000]
```

Use the following code example in order to get a better (readable) outcome to analyze the data points and the centroids they are assigned to:

```
Reader reader = new SequenceFile.Reader(fs,new Path(output,
Cluster.CLUSTERED_POINTS_DIR + "/part-m-00000"), conf);
IntWritable key = new IntWritable();
WeightedPropertyVectorWritable value = new
WeightedPropertyVectorWritable();
while (reader.next(key, value)) {
   System.out.println("key: " + key.toString()+ " value: "+
   value.toString());
}
reader.close();
```

The following image shows the outcome of the preceding code example:

```
key: 0 value: wt: 1.0 distance: 3.0   vec: 2 = [22.000, 80.000]
key: 0 value: wt: 1.0 distance: 5.0   vec: 2 = [25.000, 75.000]
key: 0 value: wt: 1.0 distance: 5.830951894845301  vec: 2 = [28.000, 85.000]
key: 2 value: wt: 1.0 distance: 2.4267032964268394  vec: 2 = [55.000, 150.000]
key: 2 value: wt: 1.0 distance: 5.088112507491256  vec: 2 = [50.000, 145.000]
key: 2 value: wt: 1.0 distance: 3.6817870057290776  vec: 2 = [53.000, 153.000]
```

After you run the algorithm, you will see the clustering output generated for each iteration and the final result in the filesystem (in the output directory you have specified; in this case, Kmeansoutput) as shown here:

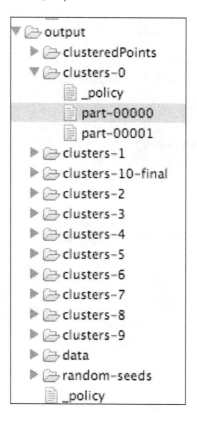

Cluster visualization

You can use the DisplayKMeans.java class in org.apache.mahout.clustering. display to visualize the clusters generated by the K-Means algorithm, as shown in the following image:

 Refer to https://mahout.apache.org/users/clustering/ visualizing-sample-clusters.html for more information.

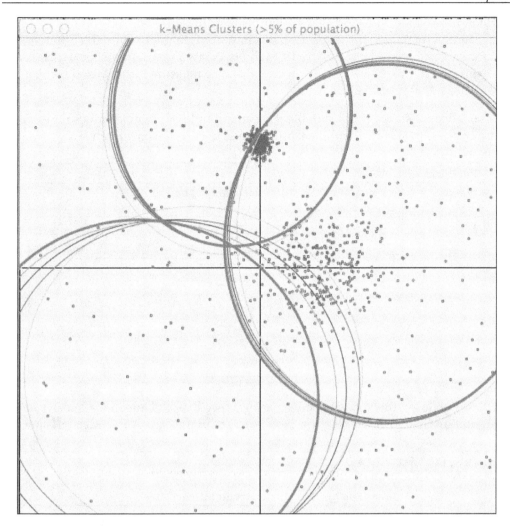

Distance measure

The clustering problem is based on evaluating the distance between data points. The distance measure is an indicator of the similarity of the data points. For any clustering algorithm, you need to make a decision on the appropriate distance measure for your context. Essentially, the distance measure is more important for accuracy than the number of clusters.

Further, the criteria for choosing the right distance measure depends on the application domain and the dataset, so it is important to understand the different distance measures available in Apache Mahout. A few important distance measures are explained in the following section. The distance measure is visualized using a two-dimensional visualization here.

The Euclidean distance is not suitable if the magnitude of possible values for each feature varies drastically (if all the features need to be assessed equally):

Euclidean distance	
Class	`org.apache.mahout.common.distance.EuclideanDistanceMeasure`
Formula	$$d = \sqrt{(a_1 - b_1)^2 + (a_2 - b_2)^2 + \cdots + (a_n - b_n)^2}$$

Squared Euclidean distance has better performance than Euclidean distance. It saves computation time by not taking the square root as in the case of Euclidean distance:

Squared Euclidean distance	
Class	`org.apache.mahout.common.distance.SquaredEuclideanDistanceMeasure`
Formula	$$d = (a_1 - b_1)^2 + (a_2 - b_2)^2 + \cdots (a_n - b_n)^2$$

Cosine distance is mostly suitable for text clustering. It disregards the length of the vectors:

Cosine distance	
Class	`org.apache.mahout.common.distance.` `CosineDistanceMeasure`
Formula	$$d = 1 - \frac{\left(a_1 b_1 + a_2 b_2 + \cdots + a_n b_n\right)}{\left(\sqrt{\left(a_1^2 + a_2^2 + \cdots + a_n^2\right)}\sqrt{\left(b_1^2 + b_2^2 + \cdots + b_n^2\right)}\right)}$$
	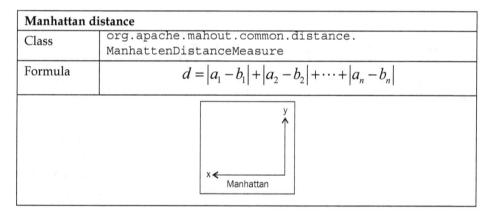

Manhattan distance is easy to generalize to higher dimensions:

Manhattan distance	
Class	`org.apache.mahout.common.distance.` `ManhattenDistanceMeasure`
Formula	$$d = \left|a_1 - b_1\right| + \left|a_2 - b_2\right| + \cdots + \left|a_n - b_n\right|$$

Tanimoto distance is also known as Jaccard distance. It captures information about the relative distance between two points and their angle:

Tanimoto distance	
Class	`org.apache.mahout.common.distance.` `TanimotoDistanceMeasure`
Formula	$$d = 1 - \frac{\left(a_1 b_1 + a_2 b_2 + \cdots + a_n b_n\right)}{\left(\sqrt{\left(a_1^2 + a_2^2 + \cdots + a_n^2\right)} + \sqrt{\left(b_1^2 + b_2^2 + \cdots + b_n^2\right)}\right) - \left(a_1 b_1 + a_2 b_2 + \cdots + a_n b_n\right)}$$

Weighted distance measure gives weights for different dimensions to evaluate similarity:

Weighted distance	
Class	`org.apache.mahout.common.distance.WeightedEuclideanDistanceMeasure`
	`org.apache.mahout.common.distance.WeightedManhattanDistanceMeasure`

Writing a custom distance measure

If the distance measures that are already available in Apache Mahout do not suit your problem domain, then you can come up with your own custom distance measures by following these steps:

- Implement the `org.apache.mahout.common.distance.DistanceMeasure` interface

- Provide custom distance logic in the distance (`Vector v1` and `Vector v2`) method

K-Means clustering with MapReduce

The key strength of Apache Mahout lies in its ability to scale. This is achieved by implementing machine learning algorithms according to the MapReduce programming paradigm.

If your dataset is small and fits into memory, then you can run Mahout in local mode. If your dataset is growing and it comes to a point where it can't fit into memory, then you should consider moving the computation to the Hadoop cluster. The complete guide on Hadoop installation is given in *Chapter 5, Apache Mahout in Production.*

In this section, we will explain how the K-Means algorithm is implemented in Apache Mahout in a scalable manner.

However, please note that it is not mandatory for you to thoroughly understand the MapReduce concept in order to use the algorithms in your applications. So, you can proceed with this section only if you are interested in understanding the internals.

Let's continue with the previous people size example, with height and weight as features. The data distribution (**d1, d2, d3**, and **d4**) and the initial centroids selected (**c1, c2**, and **c3**) are shown in the following image:

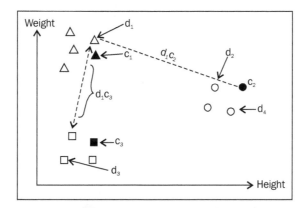

MapReduce in Apache Mahout

In Apache Mahout, MapReduce tasks are implemented on top of the Apache Hadoop framework. The `org.apache.hadoop.mapreduce.Job` class handles the distribution of tasks across multiple nodes (distributed computation). HDFS is used to handle storage distribution.

When implementing the K-Means algorithm, the MapReduce phase is used iteratively until the given termination criteria (until convergence or until a given number of iterations) is reached.

The Hadoop job segments the data points into independent HDFS blocks, which are processed by map tasks in a parallel way. In this scenario, assume that the dataset is segmented across nodes in the cluster by assigning **d1** and **d2** to node 1 and **d3** and **d4** to node 2, as shown in the following image:

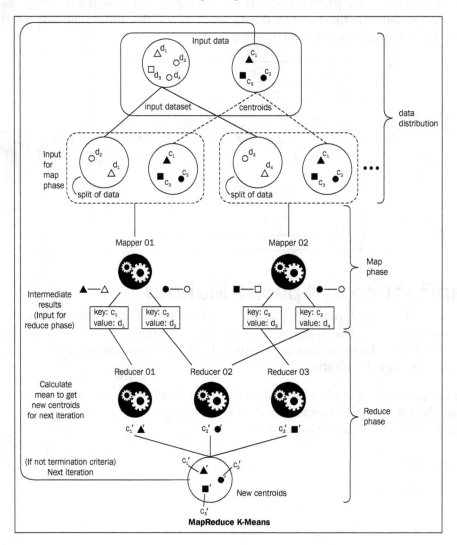

The map function

Datasets (d1 and d2 for node 1, and d3 and d4 for node 2) and initial centroids (c1, c2, and c3) are given as input to the map phase in the sequence file format.

During the map phase, distance is computed from each data point to all the initial centroids, and the data point is assigned to the closest centroid in order to find the associativity of the data points to the clusters. For example, d1c1 is less than d1c3 and d2c2, so d1 is assigned to c1 as the intermediate result of the map phase.

The output is given as a key-value pair (key = centroid id and value = data point) to the reduce phase.

The reduce function

The data points that belong to a particular centroid are processed in a single node in the reduce phase. For example, intermediate results from the map phase (c2, d4 and c2, d2) are processed in node 2.

During the reduce phase, centroid points are recalculated using the average of the coordinates of all data points in that cluster. The related data points are averaged out to produce the new position of the centroid.

The new centroids are then fed back to the next iteration as the centroid vector.

Additional clustering algorithms

The K-Means algorithm is a simple and fast algorithm for clustering. However, this algorithm has its own limitations in certain scenarios. So, we will explain other clustering algorithms that are available in Apache Mahout here.

Canopy clustering

The accuracy of the K-Means algorithm depends on the number of clusters (K) and the initial cluster points that we randomly generated.

K-Means used org.apache.mahout.clustering.kmeans.RandomSeedGenerator to determine initial clusters randomly. However, with this approach, there is no guarantee about the time to converge, so it might take a long time for a large dataset to converge. Sometimes, premature convergence may occur due to the inability to pass a local optimum.

As a solution, canopy clustering is used with K-Means clustering as the initial step to determine the initial centroids (without getting initial centroids randomly). This will speed up the clustering process for the K-Means algorithm and provide more accurate initial centroids. The execution steps for canopy clustering are given as follows:

1. Define two distance thresholds, namely **T1** and **T2**, where **T1 > T2**.

2. Remove one data point from the dataset to be clustered to form a new canopy (this is the current centroid).

3. Evaluate the remaining data points in the dataset iteratively, as follows:

    ° If the distance from the selected remaining data point to the current centroid (**d**) is less than **T1**, then assign it to the canopy

    ° If **d** is also less than **T2**, then remove the data point from the dataset, as it cannot be a centroid itself

    ° If **d** is greater than **T1**, then it is not a member of the canopy

These are some important parameters:

- **T1, T2**: These denote the distance thresholds as shown in the following image:

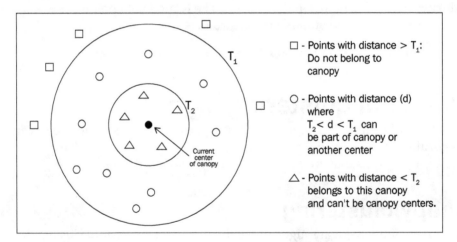

The following is the code example. Please refer to the code example for the K-Means algorithm for the complete Java code that includes input preparation and displaying the outcome:

```
// Run Canopy to get initial clusters
Path canopyOutput = new Path(output, "canopies");
CanopyDriver.run(new Configuration(),
directoryContainingConvertedInput, canopyOutput, measure, t1, t2,
false, 0.0, false);
```

```
// Run K-Means using the initial clusters found using Canopy algorithm
KMeansDriver.run(conf, directoryContainingConvertedInput, new
Path(canopyOutput, Cluster.INITIAL_CLUSTERS_DIR + "-final"),
output, convergenceDelta, maxIterations, true, 0.0, false);
```

However, this algorithm has been deprecated in Mahout v0.10, so if you want to use this refer to the prior version (v0.9).

For more information, refer to `https://mahout.apache.org/users/clustering/canopy-clustering.html`.

Fuzzy K-Means

The K-Means algorithm is for hard clustering. In hard clustering, one data point belongs only to one cluster. However, there can be situations where one point belongs to more than one cluster. For example, a news article may belong to both the *Technology* and *Current Affairs* categories. In that case, we need a soft clustering mechanism.

The Fuzzy K-Means algorithm implements soft clustering. It generates overlapping clusters. Each point has a probability of belonging to each cluster, based on the distance from each centroid.

The steps that need to be performed in order to implement Fuzzy K-Means clustering are as follows:

1. Initialize the K clusters.
2. For each data point, find the probability of data points that belong to a cluster.
3. Recompute the cluster's centroid based on the probability membership values of the data points to the clusters.
4. Iterate until convergence or a given termination criteria is met.

In this example, we apply the Fuzzy K-Means algorithm for a similar dataset as that used in the K-Means example (the size distribution of people, represented as their weights and heights) with one additional data point (`38`, `115`) to represent someone who had medium weight and height, as shown in the following image.

Save the following details as `fuzzykmeans.data` in the `fuzzykmeanstest` directory:

```
22 80
25 75
28 85
55 150
```

```
50 145
53 153
38 115
```

The following is the source code for the preceding example; please note that input preparation and displaying the outcome with the clusterdump utility is similar to that used in the K-Means algorithm and hence has been excluded to avoid duplicate code:

```
FuzzyKMeansDriver.run(conf, directoryContainingConvertedInput,
clusters, output, convergenceDelta, maxIterations,2F, true, false,
0, false);
```

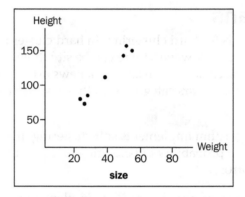

Some important parameters are:

- M – fuzzy ness argument: If m is closer to 1, the cluster center closest to the point considered is given more weight

- `emitMostLikely`: This emits the most likely cluster that the cluster point belongs to

The outcome of the preceding code example is given in the following figure. Note that the newly added data point (someone who had medium weight and height) belongs to cluster 3 in 0.52 probability and to cluster 1 in 0.47 probability, whereas other data points (people who are either large or small) belongs to nearly 0.9 to a particular cluster.

```
key: 3 value: wt: 7.901409108580251E-5 distance: 4910.017900330829  vec: 2 = [22.000, 80.000]
key: 1 value: wt: 0.9999209859089142 distance: 43.64681000770361  vec: 2 = [22.000, 80.000]
key: 3 value: wt: 3.116092454827647E-4 distance: 5414.081428263446  vec: 2 = [25.000, 75.000]
key: 1 value: wt: 0.9996883907545173 distance: 95.58673474894567  vec: 2 = [25.000, 75.000]
key: 3 value: wt: 2.0009177743743571E-7 distance: 3989.5493415962883  vec: 2 = [28.000, 85.000]
key: 1 value: wt: 0.9999997999082225 distance: 1.7845902059006105  vec: 2 = [28.000, 85.000]
key: 3 value: wt: 0.9998763642180029 distance: 56.41991925815819  vec: 2 = [55.000, 150.000]
key: 1 value: wt: 1.2363578199703958E-4 distance: 5073.802071458969  vec: 2 = [55.000, 150.000]
key: 3 value: wt: 0.9999999352240232 distance: 1.0656967924836704  vec: 2 = [50.000, 145.000]
key: 1 value: wt: 6.477597677891038E-8 distance: 4187.22848069849  vec: 2 = [50.000, 145.000]
key: 3 value: wt: 0.9997387238423375 distance: 86.7463587386228  vec: 2 = [53.000, 153.000]
key: 1 value: wt: 2.6127615766246854E-4 distance: 5365.925278726681  vec: 2 = [53.000, 153.000]
key: 3 value: wt: 0.5252817730427746 distance: 998.1303003946014  vec: 2 = [38.000, 115.000]
key: 1 value: wt: 0.4747182269572255 distance: 1049.942346014479  vec: 2 = [38.000, 115.000]
```

For more information on the Fuzzy K-Means algorithm, refer to `https://mahout.apache.org/users/clustering/fuzzy-k-means.html`.

Streaming K-Means

If the volume of data is too large to be stored in the main memory available, the K-Means algorithm is not suitable, as it's batch processing mechanism iterates over all the data points. Also, the K-Means algorithm is sensitive to the noise and outliers in data. Moreover, its random initialization step causes problems when it comes to computation time and accuracy.

Streaming K-Means algorithms has provided a solution for these problems by operating in two steps, as follows:

*   The streaming step
*   The ball K-Means step

The idea is to read data points sequentially, storing very few data points in memory. Then, after the first step, a better representative set of weighted data points is produced for further processing. The final K number of clusters is produced in the ball K-Means step. During the second step, potential outliers are eliminated.

The streaming step

During the streaming step, the algorithm makes only one pass through the data and evaluates the data points as follows:

1. Select a data point randomly as the initial centroid (**c1**).

2. If **d1** is a new point and **c1** is the closest cluster to **d1**, measure the distance between **d1** and **c1** (**d1c1**):

    1. If **d1c1** is smaller than the `distanceCutoff` parameter, then assign the data point to **c1**.

    2. If **d1c1** is greater than the `distanceCutoff`, then create a new cluster with the data point.

3. For all the data points, follow the preceding steps.

4. This step will roughly cluster the input data points and obtain a set of weighted clusters for the ball K-Means step.

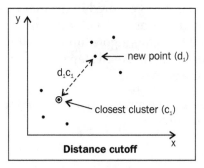

The following are some important parameters to consider for the streaming step:

1. `numClusters`: This is an approximate value of the number of clusters produced in the streaming K-Means step. This is not the final number of clusters generated by the algorithm, and this number is subject to change.

2. `distanceCutoff`: This is a parameter that represents the value of the distance between a point and its closest centroid, after which the new point will definitely be assigned to a new cluster. This parameter will influence the number of clusters generated during this step.

3. `beta` (double): This is a constant parameter that controls the growth of `distanceCutoff`.

4. `clusterLogFactor`: This is a runtime estimation of the number of clusters produced by the streaming step.

5. `clusterOvershoot`: This is a constant multiplicative slack factor that slows down the collapsing of clusters.

The ball K-Means step

The ball K-Means step is used to refine the outcome of the streaming step and to get the number of clusters required.

1. First, determine the initial centroids using K-Means++ or random mechanism.

2. Then, assign the data points to their closest clusters.

3. Trim the clusters. If the distance from the data point to its closest cluster is greater than the distance from the closest cluster to another cluster, then eliminate that data point as an outlier using the trim fraction. For example, if **d1c1** > `trimFraction`* **c1c2**, then eliminate the **d1** point in the following.

4. Form new centroids using trimmed clusters.

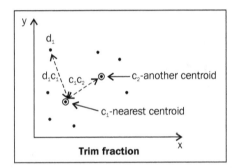

The following are some important parameters for the ball K-Means step:

- `trimFraction`: This parameter is used to eliminate outliers.

- `kMeansPlusPlusInit`: If `true`, the seeding method is K-Means++. If `false`, the seeding method is used to select points uniformly at random.

- `correctWeights`: If `correctWeights` is true, outliers will be considered when calculating the weight of centroids.

- `numRuns` (`int`): This is the number of runs to perform.

Spectral clustering

The spectral clustering algorithm is helpful in hard, nonconvex clustering problems. It clusters points using the **eigenvectors** of matrices derived from data.

For more information, check out `http://mahout.apache.org/users/clustering/spectral-clustering.html`.

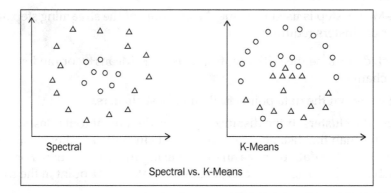

Spectral vs. K-Means

The command-line example can be found at `https://mahout.apache.org/users/clustering/spectral-clustering.html`.

Dirichlet clustering

The Fuzzy K-Means and K-Means algorithms model clusters as spheres (circles in n-dimensional space.) K-Means assumes a common fixed variance. Further, K-Means does not model the data point distribution.

A normal data distribution should be there for the K-Means and Fuzzy K-Means algorithms to process effectively. If the data distribution is different, for example, an asymmetrical normal distribution (different standard deviations), the K-Means algorithm will not perform well and will not give good results.

Dirichlet clustering can be applied to model different data distributions (data points that are not in normal distribution) effectively. Dirichlet clustering fits a model over a dataset and tunes parameters to adjust the model's parameters to correctly fit the data. This approach is suitable to address the hierarchical-clustering problem. However, Apache Mahout's Dirichlet implementation is deprecated now and is not included after v8.0.

Example scripts for different clustering algorithms can be found at the following locations:

- `MAHOUT_HOME/ examples/ bin/cluster-reuters.sh` (The K-Means, Fuzzy K-Means, LDA, and streaming K-Means algorithms)
- `MAHOUT_HOME/ examples/ bin/cluster-syntheticcontrol.sh` (canopy, K-Means, Fuzzy K-Means)

Text clustering

Text clustering is a widely used application of clustering that is used in areas such as records, management systems, searches, and business intelligence.

The vector space model and TF-IDF

In text clustering, the terms of the documents are considered as features in text clustering. The vector space model is an algebraic model that maps the terms in a document into n-dimensional linear space.

However, we need to represent textual information (terms) as a numerical representation and create feature vectors using the numerical values to evaluate the similarity between data points.

Each dimension of the feature vector represents a separate term. If a particular term is present in the document, then the vector value is set using the **Term Frequency (TF)** or **Term Frequency-Inverse Document Frequency (TF-IDF)** calculation. TF indicates the frequency at which the term appears in a given document. TF-IDF is an improved way of TF, which indicates how important a word to a document.

In order to facilitate the preceding concept, Apache Mahout uses the following classes:

- `org.apache.mahout.vectorizer.DictionaryVectorizer.createTermFrequencyVector`
- `org.apache.mahout.vectorizer.tfidf.TFIDFConverter.calculateDF`
- `org.apache.mahout.vectorizer.tfidf.TFIDFConverter.processTfIdf`

N-grams and collocations

Even though we consider individual terms as features for clustering, there are situations where certain terms co-occur frequently and can be considered as a single term (for example, machine learning).

Apache Mahout provides a sound way to handle this issue with the N-gram concept during term vector creation. By default, bigrams are considered and you can change this using the configuration value for `maxNGramSize`.

For more details about N-grams and collocations in Apache Mahout, read `https://mahout.apache.org/users/basics/collocations.html`.

Preprocessing text with Lucene

As a preprocessing step, we first need to tokenize the document using the following method in Apache Mahout:

- `org.apache.mahout.vectorizer.DocumentProcessor.tokenizeDocuments`

During tokenization, we need to decide on the other text preprocessing steps.

Before generating term vectors, Apache Mahout applies some text preprocessing steps, such as stop word removal, lower case removal, and length-based filtering to improve the accuracy of the end result and reduce computation time, using `org.apache.lucene.analysis.Analyzer`.

The following image shows a detailed example that demonstrates the vector space, TF-IDF, and preprocessing concepts:

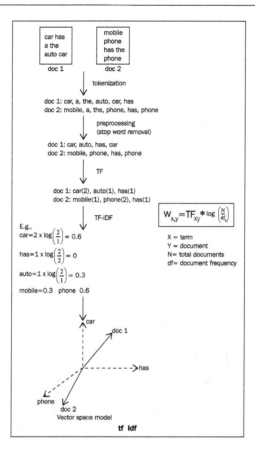

Generated TF-IDF vectors are given as input to the K-Means algorithm or any preferred clustering algorithm.

Text clustering with the K-Means algorithm

The following example demonstrates text document clustering using the K-Means algorithm in the command line. Wikipedia content is given in the text documents. The files are copied to HDFS and processed with Hadoop MapReduce.

A step-by-step guide to Hadoop installation is provided in *Chapter 5, Apache Mahout in Production,* so please refer to that guide in order to set up the Hadoop environment. You can try out the commands in local mode as well. To do this, perform the following steps:

1. Copy the files from the local filesystem folder to HDFS:

```
hdfs dfs -put kmeans/input/ kmeans/input
```

2. Use the following command to display the copied files, as shown in the image that follows:

```
hdfs dfs -ls kmeans/input
```

```
-rw-r--r--   2 hduser supergroup        807 2015-05-01 05:17 kmeans/input/cricket
-rw-r--r--   2 hduser supergroup        869 2015-05-01 05:17 kmeans/input/football
-rw-r--r--   2 hduser supergroup        739 2015-05-01 05:17 kmeans/input/kamelot
-rw-r--r--   2 hduser supergroup       1392 2015-05-01 05:17 kmeans/input/nightwish
```

3. Convert the input to sequence files:

```
mahout seqdirectory -i kmeans/input/ -o kmeans/sequencefiles
```

4. Use the preceding command to display sequence files, as shown in the following image:

```
hdfs dfs -text kmeans/sequencefiles/part-m-00000
```

 Note that the filename is taken as the key, and the file's content is taken as the value for each document in a sequence file.

```
/cricket        Cricket is a bat-and-ball game played between two teams of 11 players each on a field at the centre of which is a rec
tangular 22-yard long pitch. The game is played by 120 million players in many countries, making it the world's second most popular s
port.[1][2][3] Each team takes its turn to bat, attempting to score runs, while the other team fields. Each turn is known as an innin
gs.

The bowler delivers the ball to the batsman who attempts to hit the ball with his bat away from the fielders so he can run to the oth
er end of the pitch and score a run. Each batsman continues batting until he is out. The batting team continues batting until ten bat
smen are out, or a specified number of overs of six balls have been bowled, at which point the teams switch roles and the fielding te
am comes in to bat.

/football       American football (referred to as football in the United States and also known as gridiron) is a sport played by two
teams of eleven players on a rectangular field with goalposts at each end. The offense, the team with control of the oval-shaped foot
ball, attempts to advance down the field by running with or passing the ball, while the team without control of the ball, the defense
, aims to stop their advance and take control of the ball for themselves. The offense must advance at least ten yards in four downs,
or plays, or else they turn over the football to the opposing team; if they succeed, they are given a new set of four downs. Points a
re primarily scored by advancing the ball into the opposing team's end zone for a touchdown or kicking the ball through the opponent'
s goalposts for a field goal. The team with the most points at the end of a game wins.

/kamelot        Kamelot is an American power metal band from Tampa, Florida, formed by Thomas Youngblood and Richard Warner in 1991.
The Norwegian vocalist Roy Khan joined for the album Si?ge Perilous, and shared songwriting credit with Youngblood until his departur
e in April 2011. On June 22, 2012, Youngblood announced on their website that their new vocalist is the Swedish singer Tommy Karevik,
who is featured on Kamelot's latest album Silverthorn as main vocalist, co songwriter and lyricist.

Up until 2012, Kamelot had released ten studio albums (excluding two reissues), two live albums, one live DVD, and seven music videos
. Their latest studio album is Silverthorn, which was released October 2012 via SPV/Steamhammer and King Records Japan.

/nightwish      Nightwish is a symphonic metal band from Kitee, Finland. The band was formed in 1996 by lead songwriter and keyboardi
st Tuomas Holopainen, guitarist Emppu Vuorinen, and lead singer Tarja Turunen. The band soon picked up drummer Jukka Nevalainen, and
then bassist Sami V?nsk? after the release of its debut album, Angels Fall First (1997). In 2002, V?nsk? was replaced by Marco Hietal
a, who also took over the male vocalist role previously filled by Holopainen or guest singers.[1]

Although Nightwish have been prominent in their home country since Angels Fall First, they did not achieve worldwide fame until the r
elease of the albums Oceanborn (1998), Wishmaster (2000) and Century Child (2002). Their 2004 album, Once, has sold more than one mil
lion copies[2] and was the band's breakthrough in the United States. Their biggest US hit single, Wish I Had an Angel (2004), receive
d MTV airplay and was included on three US film soundtracks to promote their North American tour.[3][4] The band produced three more
singles and two music videos for Once, as well as a re-recording of ?Sleeping Sun?for the ?best of?compilation album, Highest Hopes (
2005), before Turunen's dismissal in October 2005.[3] Her last performance with Nightwish was recorded on the live album/DVD End of a
n Era; after the show, the other members announced to Turunen that she was no longer a member of Nightwish.
```

5. Generate TF-IDF vectors from sequence files:

```
mahout seq2sparse -i kmeans/sequencefiles -o kmeans/sparse
```

The outcome and intermediate results during the TF-IDF vector creation are shown in the following image:

```
drwxr-xr-x   - hduser supergroup          0 2015-05-01 05:31 kmeans/sparse/df-count
-rw-r--r--   2 hduser supergroup       1872 2015-05-01 05:30 kmeans/sparse/dictionary.file-0
-rw-r--r--   2 hduser supergroup       2073 2015-05-01 05:31 kmeans/sparse/frequency.file-0
drwxr-xr-x   - hduser supergroup          0 2015-05-01 05:31 kmeans/sparse/tf-vectors
drwxr-xr-x   - hduser supergroup          0 2015-05-01 05:32 kmeans/sparse/tfidf-vectors
drwxr-xr-x   - hduser supergroup          0 2015-05-01 05:29 kmeans/sparse/tokenized-documents
drwxr-xr-x   - hduser supergroup          0 2015-05-01 05:30 kmeans/sparse/wordcount
```

6. Execute the K-Means algorithm, as shown here:

    ```
    mahout kmeans -i kmeans/sparse/tfidf-vectors/ -c kmeans/
    cl -o kmeans/out -dm org.apache.mahout.common.distance.
    CosineDistanceMeasure -x 10 -k 2 --clustering -cl
    ```

    The outcome directory, which is kmeans.out in this case, will contain the files shown in the following image:

```
-rw-r--r--   2 hduser supergroup        194 2015-05-01 05:36 kmeans/out/_policy
drwxr-xr-x   - hduser supergroup          0 2015-05-01 05:36 kmeans/out/clusteredPoints
drwxr-xr-x   - hduser supergroup          0 2015-05-01 05:35 kmeans/out/clusters-0
drwxr-xr-x   - hduser supergroup          0 2015-05-01 05:36 kmeans/out/clusters-1-final
```

7. Display the results of the K-Means clustering:

    ```
    mahout clusterdump -dt sequencefile -d kmeans/sparse/dictionary.
    file-0 -i kmeans/out/clusters-1-final
    ```

    The outcome of the clusterdump command is shown in the following image; the image shows the terms that belong to each cluster with their associated weights and the top terms for each cluster:

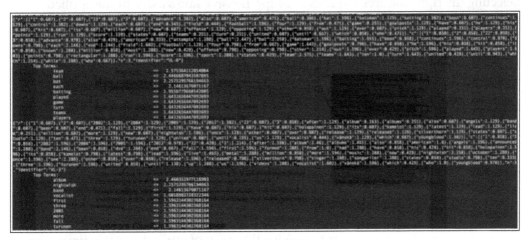

Result of the clusterdump command

More details on the clusterdumper tool can be found at `https://mahout.apache.org/users/clustering/cluster-dumper.html`.

Only the required command-line options are given for the preceding commands. Please refer to Mahout command-line help for complete reference.

Topic modeling

Topic modeling (Latent Dirichlet Allocation – CVB) is one way of implementing clustering for a text document collection. This technique is widely applied to categorize Google news and reviews.

In topic modeling, each document is represented as a distribution of topics (the doc-topic distribution). And essentially, a topic is a probability distribution over words (the topic-term distribution).

More details on topic modeling can be found at `http://jayaniwithanawasam.blogspot.com/2013/12/infer-topics-for-documents-using-latent.html`.

Optimizing clustering performance

Developing a clustering algorithm without having any programming errors may not give you the expected results. There are many factors to consider based on the application's context and the requirements.

Selecting the right features

Selecting the right features requires a comprehensive knowledge of the applied domain. You can ensure that you select the right features to accurately represent the problem domain using the following techniques:

- Selecting and weighing features properly
- Normalizing dimensions when values are not comparable (For example, the number of bedrooms in a house and the land price in dollars are not comparable in their innate forms.)
- Using effective preprocessing mechanisms (custom Lucene analyzers and noise reduction)
- Selecting the suitable vector representation (`SequentialAccessSparseVector`, `RandomAccessSparseVector` or `DenseVector`)
- Normalizing data points to remove the effect of outliers in each dimension

Selecting the right algorithms

An algorithm should be selected so that it naturally solves the given problem. For example, if your data does not fit into the normal distribution, then you might not need to consider the K-Means algorithm.

Selecting the right distance measure

Cluster quality is also dependent on the measure used to calculate the similarity between two feature vectors.

Apache Mahout already provides a number of distance measures. You need to carefully select the distance measure that best represents the problem of these distance measures.

If none of the existing distance measures satisfy the requirement at hand, implement a custom distance measure.

Evaluating clusters

You need to ensure that high intracluster similarity and low intercluster similarity are present once clustering is completed. This is achieved by measuring intercluster distance and intracluster distance.

The initialization of centroids and the number of clusters

You can try multiple random initializations before finalizing the initial centroids to avoid K-Means getting stuck in local optima.

The `cost` function can be used to decide the optimal number of clusters. The number of clusters can be decided by focusing on the purpose of clustering as well.

The initialization of centroids to optimal values is important to reduce the execution time by having fewer iterations.

Tuning up parameters

The use of machine learning algorithms frequently involves the careful tuning of learning parameters. If the K-Means algorithm takes longer than expected to converge, then you can tune the convergence delta and the number of iterations to find the optimal value for these parameters that gives reasonable results. The values are chosen mostly by trial and error.

The decision on infrastructure

Ideally, increasing the number of the nodes should reduce the execution time. However, for small datasets, it can result in the under utilization of computation resources.

The following is a small checklist that you can use to ensure the quality of the clustering application:

- Did you select a distance measure that correctly distinguishes chosen features?
- Did you select the correct algorithm that is capable of clustering by accurately considering the distribution of the dataset?
- Did you make some effort to improve the weights or the scale of the better features relative to the features that are not discriminating well?

Summary

Clustering is an unsupervised learning mechanism that requires minimal human effort. Clustering has many applications in different areas, such as medical image processing, market segmentation, and information retrieval.

Clustering mechanisms can be divided into different types, such as hard, soft, flat, hierarchical, and model-based clustering based on different criteria.

Apache Mahout implements different clustering algorithms, which can be accessed sequentially or in parallel (using MapReduce).

The K-Means algorithm is a simple and fast algorithm that is widely applied. However, there are situations that the K-Means algorithm will not be able to cater to. For such scenarios, Apache Mahout has implemented other algorithms, such as canopy, Fuzzy K-Means, streaming, and spectral clustering.

Text clustering is an important area of clustering that requires special preprocessing steps, such as stop word removal, stemming, and TF-IDF vector generation. Topic modeling is a special case of text clustering.

There are several techniques that can be used to optimize cluster performance to get expected results, such as selecting the right features, distance measures, and algorithms, to name a few.

3
Regression and Classification

This chapter explains the regression and classification technique in machine learning and its implementation using different machine learning algorithms in Apache Mahout. The machine learning theory behind the algorithm and real-world applications with example scripts are also explained.

In this chapter, we will cover the following topics:

- Supervised learning
- Target variables and predictor variables
- Predictive analytics techniques
- Classification versus regression
- Linear regression with Apache Spark
- Logistic regression with Stochastic Gradient Descent (SGD)
- Naïve Bayes algorithm
- Hidden Markov Models (HMMs)

Supervised learning

Supervised learning is a machine learning technique that requires labeled training data.

In supervised learning, algorithms model the relationship between features and labels during the learning phase. The training algorithm uses a known dataset (called the training dataset) to make predictions.

The data (including observations, measurements, and so on) is labeled with predefined classes.

For example, let's say we are given a collection of balls of different sizes with category labels such as big and small attached to them; we should be able to categorize them using supervised learning by considering their attributes, such as radius and label values.

Target variables and predictor variables

There are two types of variables in classification and regression, as follows:

- **Target variables**: These are the variables that should be the output
- **Predictor variables**: These are the observations or the variables that are mapped to the target variable

The target variable represents the output or effect. The predictor variables represent the input or cause.

For example, in a loan approval scenario, the decision on approval (yes or no) is the target variable.

The characteristics or features that the previous decision is based on, such as age, marital status, outstanding debts, and annual salary are predictor variables.

The target variable is also known as the dependent variable. Predictor variables are also known as independent variables.

Predictive analytics' techniques

There are different types of predictive analytics techniques based on the method of analysis. The nature of the learning input and predicted outcome remains the same for all the techniques, which are explained in the sections that follow.

Regression-based prediction

Regression-based prediction is predicting the unknown value of a variable from the known value of another variable. We predict scores on one variable based on the scores of a second (or more) variable.

There are two methods of regression that are based on the outcome/target variable:

- Linear regression
- Logistic regression

An example of regression-based prediction is **Stochastic Gradient Descent (SGD)**.

Model-based prediction

In model-based prediction, we assume that the data follows a specific statistic model. By following this method, we can take advantage of the structure of the data by building a parametric model for a given data distribution.

An example of model-based prediction is Naïve Bayes.

Tree-based prediction

A tree-based prediction iteratively splits the outcome to different groups. It evaluates the similarity of outcomes in each group.

This method is relatively simple and easy. This has better performance in nonlinear settings. However, it is hard to work with tree-based prediction in uncertain situations.

Some examples of tree-based prediction are decision trees and random forests.

Classification versus regression

Methods for prediction can be divided into two general groups, based on the outcome of the prediction algorithm, as follows:

- When the data is **discrete**, we will refer to it as **classification**. Discriminant analysis and pattern recognition are the other similar terms used for classification.
- When the data is **continuous**, we will refer to it as **regression**. Other terms used for regression are smoothing and curve estimation.

Linear regression with Apache Spark

Linear regression is the most commonly used method for describing the relationship between predictors (or covariates) and outcomes.

Linear regression can solve problems that require a continuous target variable to predict real, valued outcomes. There can be multiple variables or features in the problem domain.

How does linear regression work?

Linear regression focuses on finding optimal values for parameters (coefficients) to fit the best possible hyper plane to the training data.

Linear regression is approached as a minimization problem. The mean squared error, which is the difference between the expected outcome and the actual outcome for the training set, is minimized.

The squared error function is also known as the cost function. So, the goal is to minimize the cost function.

Each value of the parameter given in the cost function refers to one hypothesis function. The idea is to find the optimal hypothesis that has values for parameters which best minimize the cost function.

A real-world example

Now, let's go through a real-world scenario to further understand this algorithm and implement it using Apache Mahout.

The impact of smoking on mortality and different diseases

During observational studies using regression analysis, it has been found that tobacco smoking can cause mortality and diseases, such as bronchitis and emphysema.

Linear regression helps you to perform data analysis and come up with observations or insights, as follows:

- The impact of the socioeconomic status of a person, such as income and education, on mortality or diverse diseases
- The risk of mortality or getting different diseases for smokers
- The relationship between the number of cigarettes consumed per day and mortality
- The relationship between the number of cigarettes consumed per day and having different diseases, such as bronchitis and emphysema

An example outcome of linear regression analysis with one variable or observation (cigarette smoking frequency) is shown in the following image.

After the analysis, it is evident that a higher cigarette smoking frequency has a higher risk of mortality.

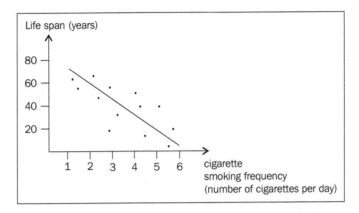

Linear regression with one variable and multiple variables

The following table contains some sample data on the impact of cigarette smoking on lifespan. Lifespan can be affected by several other factors such as a person's socioeconomic status, in addition to smoking.

Socioeconomic status is an economic and sociological collective measure of a person's work experience and of an individual's or family's economic and social position in relation to others, based on income, education, and occupation (refer to http://en.wikipedia.org/wiki/Socioeconomic_status for more information regarding this).

Here, we can consider the cigarette smoking frequency and socioeconomic status (SES) as predictor variables and lifespan as the target variable.

We represent the socioeconomic status on a scale of 1 to 10, where 1 represents the lowest SES and 10 represents the highest SES.

The following image shows the preceding scenario modeled in linear regression:

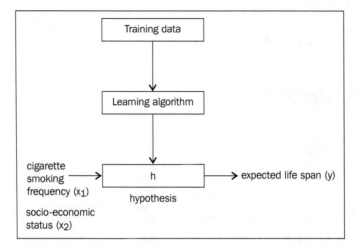

The following table shows the impact of cigarette smoking on lifespan:

Cigarette smoking frequency (per day) (x1)	Socioeconomic status (x2)	Lifespan (years) (y)
10	2	43
20	1	30
2	10	70
5	5	54
0	10	98

The following image shows a visual representation of the preceding scenario:

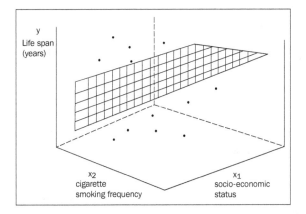

The integration of Apache Spark

In *Chapter 1, Introducing Apache Mahout,* we gave a brief introduction to Apache Spark integration with Apache Mahout and the problem that it is intended to address.

In this chapter, we will continue the linear regression code example with the integration of Apache Spark and Apache Mahout. Apache Spark's integration with Apache Mahout has been officially released with Mahout v0.10.

 If you want to know more about the integration of Apache Spark with Mahout, go to `http://www.slideshare.net/tdunning/whats-new-in-apache-mahout`.

Setting up Apache Spark with Apache Mahout

Before proceeding to the linear regression example, we need to download and set up Apache Spark with Apache Mahout by performing the following steps:

1. Download Apache Spark from `https://spark.apache.org/downloads.html`.

 The Apache Spark version you download here has to match the Apache Spark version that is mentioned in the Apache Mahout `MAHOUT_HOME/pom.xml` file as shown here:

```
<spark.version>[Version_downloaded]</spark.version>
```

2. Change the directory to the Spark downloaded directory and build using the following command:

```
sbt/sbt assembly
```

3. Switch the directory to downloaded the Spark directory and then start the Spark servers:

```
sbin/start-all.sh
```

Now, Apache Spark should be successfully running in `http://localhost:8080/`, as shown in the following screenshot. Note the URL of Spark (for example, **spark://jwithanawasam:7077** in the following screenshot):

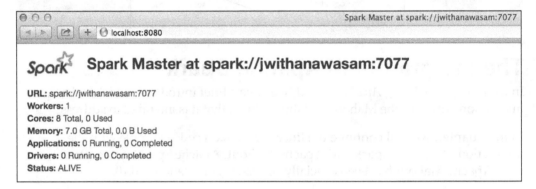

4. Set the environment variables as follows:

```
export MAHOUT_HOME=[directory into which you downloaded Mahout]
export SPARK_HOME=[directory where you unpacked Spark]
export MASTER=[url of the Spark master]
```

5. Finally, change the directory to the MAHOUT_HOME directory path and type the following commands:

```
bin/mahout spark-shell
```

```
mahout> prompt screen should appear.
```

An example script

Before continuing to the code example, let's understand a few important concepts regarding Mahout Spark integration.

Distributed row matrix

The Apache Mahout DSL has frequently used the concept of distributed memory to improve performance.

The **distributed row matrix (DRM)** is a matrix partitioned by rows and distributed in the memory of clustered computers. Matrix operations are executed on distributed memory in a parallel manner (for example, a matrix transpose).

Here's the code example for the previously mentioned scenario:

```
// Load the data
val drmData = drmParallelize(dense(
  (10, 2, 43),
  (20,   1, 30),
  (2,   10, 70),
  (5,    5, 54),
  (0,   10, 98),
  (45,   2,  20),
  (4,    4, 48),
  (7,    6, 65),
  (8,    7, 68)),
  numPartitions = 2);


// Extract target and predictor variables

val drmX = drmData(::, 0 until 2)
val y = drmData.collect(::, 2)


// Estimate the parameter vector
val drmXtX = drmX.t %*% drmX
val drmXty = drmX.t %*% y

val XtX = drmXtX.collect
val Xty = drmXty.collect(::, 0)


val beta = solve(XtX, Xty)

// Evaluation of the model
val yFitted = (drmX %*% beta).collect(::, 0)
(y - yFitted).norm(2)


// Refactored OLS function
def ols(drmX: DrmLike[Int], y: Vector) =
solve(drmX.t %*% drmX, drmX.t %*% y)(::, 0)
```

```
// Goodness of fit
def goodnessOfFit(drmX: DrmLike[Int], beta: Vector, y: Vector) = {
  val fittedY = (drmX %*% beta).collect(::, 0)
  (y - fittedY).norm(2)
}

// Adding bias term
val drmXwithBiasColumn = drmX.mapBlock(ncol = drmX.ncol + 1) {
  case(keys, block) =>

  val blockWithBiasColumn = block.like(block.nrow, block.ncol + 1)
  blockWithBiasColumn(::, 0 until block.ncol) := block
  blockWithBiasColumn(::, block.ncol) := 1

  keys -> blockWithBiasColumn
}

val betaWithBiasTerm = ols(drmXwithBiasColumn, y)
goodnessOfFit(drmXwithBiasColumn, betaWithBiasTerm, y)

val cachedDrmX = drmXwithBiasColumn.checkpoint()

val betaWithBiasTerm = ols(cachedDrmX, y)
val goodness = goodnessOfFit(cachedDrmX, betaWithBiasTerm, y)

cachedDrmX.uncache()
```

To execute the example, you need to give this code example in the Mahout shell.

An explanation of the code

The following is an explanation for the preceding code:

```
val drmData = drmParallelize(dense(
  (10, 2, 43),
  (20,   1, 30),
  (2,   10, 70),
  (5,    5, 54),
  (0,   10, 98),
  (45,   2,  20),
  (4,    4,  48),
  (7,    6,  65),
  (8,    7,  68)),
  numPartitions = 2);
```

- `drmParallelize`: This loads the dataset to the clustered environment

  In each row, give the values for the predictor variables in the first two columns and the target variable in the last column.

  For example, in the first row, 10 (cigarette smoking frequency), 2 (socioeconomic status)are predictor variable values and 43 (life span) is the value for target variable for a given instance.

- `dense`: This creates a dense matrix

  ```
  val drmX = drmData(::, 0 until 2)
  ```

  Here, we extract only the first two columns (cigarette smoking frequency and socioeconomic status), which are the predictor variables to one matrix (slicing).

  The result is a DRM. Mahout's DSL will automatically optimize and parallelize operations on DRMs and runs them on Apache Spark.

  ```
  val y = drmData.collect(::, 2)
  ```

  Then, we extract the target variable.

- `drmData.collect`: This is the fetch to memory of the driver machine's memory

  The outcome is:

  ```
  y: org.apache.mahout.math.Vector =
  {0:43.0,1:30.0,2:70.0,3:54.0,4:98.0,5:20.0,6:48.0,7:65.0,8:68.0
  }
  ```

  Estimating the parameter vector (β) is done using the **ordinary least squares** (**OLS**) method, as follows:

  β is estimated as $(X^TX)^{-1}X^Ty$
  ```
  val drmXtX = drmX.t %*% drmX
  val drmXty = drmX.t %*% y

  val XtX = drmXtX.collect
  val Xty = drmXty.collect(::, 0)
  ```

- The `.t()` operation transposes a matrix and related to R `%*%` denotes matrix multiplication

  This is the outcome for this:

  ```
  XtX: org.apache.mahout.math.Matrix =
  {
    0  =>  {0:2683.0,1:289.0}
    1  =>  {0:289.0,1:335.0}
  ```

```
}

Xty: org.apache.mahout.math.Vector = {0:3531.0,1:3164.0}

val beta = solve(XtX, Xty)
```

- `solve`: This computes the beta (the beta is a vector of unknown parameters)
  This is the outcome for this:

```
beta: org.apache.mahout.math.Vector =
{0:0.32931959905995917,1:9.160676524990066}
```

The implementation of the linear regression algorithm is completed now.

Note that all the complicated details related to distribution and parallelization are abstracted away from the user here.

The following is the evaluation of the model:

```
val yFitted = (drmX %*% beta).collect(::, 0)
(y - yFitted).norm(2)

yFitted: org.apache.mahout.math.Vector =
{0:21.614549040579725,1:15.74706850618925,2:92.265404448020
58,3:47.44998062025012,4:91.60676524990066,5:33.14073500767
8295,6:37.9599844962001,7:57.26929634336011,8:66.7592924674
1013}
```

The result is `Double = 39.68364865597313`.

- Goodness of fit:
  The goodness of fit of a statistical model explains how well the model fits a set of observations

Mahout references

You can take a look at a similar example available at `https://mahout.apache.org/users/sparkbindings/play-with-shell.html`.

The bias-variance trade-off

In this section, we will be giving a brief explanation on a few machine learning problems that can occur in practical scenarios, which might lead to inaccurate models.

The problems are listed down, as follows:

- Over-fitting
- Under-fitting

Model over-fitting and under-fitting, which is shown in the following image, can occur due to the errors caused by the bias and variance of the model. The difference between the expected prediction and the actual prediction is the error due to bias. The inconsistency of a model prediction for a given data point is the error due to variance.

Usually, there will be a trade-off between minimizing bias and variance. A low variance with high bias can lead to model under-fitting, whereas a low bias with high variance can lead to over-fitting. Accordingly, the model is unable to generalize well for new observations because it is too specific.

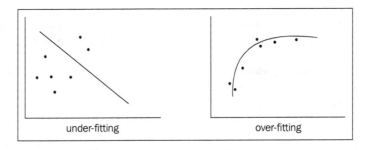

How to avoid over-fitting and under-fitting

You can perform the following steps to avoid model over-fitting and under-fitting:

1. Give an optimal number of iterations to train the model by minimizing errors (too many iterations can cause over-fitting and too few iterations can cause under-fitting).

2. Have the right number of features (too many features leads to over-fitting, as it fails to generalize new/unseen observations).

3. Have sufficient training data (too little training data along with a high number of features can lead to over-fitting).

4. Add regularization terms (keep all the features but reduce the values of the parameters).

These issues apply to logistic regression as well, which we will explain in the next section.

Logistic regression with SGD

Logistic regression solves problems that require the target variable to be a discrete value / categorical target variable. For example, a person's gender (male or female) can be a discrete output variable.

Even though a continuous outcome variable generated in linear regression can be converted to a categorical variable, it is not advisable to do so as it can drastically reduce the precision of the results.

Logistic regression can be applied in any of the following situations:

- When there is a nonlinear relationship between the predictor variables and the target variable
- When the variance of errors is not constant

The fundamental principle behind the logistic regression algorithm (using the maximum likelihood estimation) is dissimilar to that of linear regression.

In its basic form, logistic regression estimates the probability of an event occurring. Logistic regression generally uses conditional maximum likelihood estimation. Parameters (w) that make the probability of the observed (y) values of the training data the highest are selected, when (x) observations are given.

Predictor variables can be numerical or categorical. This algorithm is included only in Apache Mahout v0.9 (not in Apache Mahout v1.0).

Logistic functions

Logistic regression is built on the logistic function shown in the following image (*Logistic function*). Here, only a single input value (I) is given on the *x*.

In logistic regression, there can be multiple input variables. Moreover, it contains coefficients for each input variable.

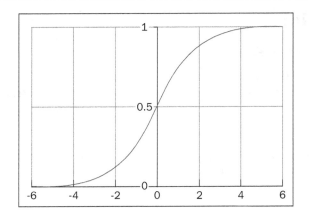

Minimizing the cost function

To classify data with high accuracy, the optimal coefficients (β) to each input variable should be assigned.

If the difference between the observed and actual probabilities (cost) is low, then we can consider the model to be accurate. We can determine the values for the coefficient (β) by minimizing the cost function.

Minimizing the cost function is achieved using SGD, which is also known as the **Online Gradient Descent**. The coefficients are updated iteratively while minimizing the cost and improving accuracy.

SGD has become popular in the machine learning community due to its scalability. SGD uses a constant amount of memory, irrespective of the input training dataset.

So, even though Mahout's SGD implementation is sequential, it claims to have a significant performance.

If the number of the training data points is large, then it is advisable to use SGD instead of **Gradient Descent (GD)** as SGD converges much faster than GD.

However, the performance of SGD comes at the cost of accuracy, as due to its stochastic nature, as error function is not minimized optimally.

This algorithm successfully pertains to large-scale and sparse machine learning problems in text classification and natural language processing.

Multinomial logistic regression versus binary logistic regression

- **Binary logistic regression**: In binary logistic regression, the dependent variable is binary. The number of available categories is restricted to two.

  Gene-based cancer classification is an example of binary logistic regression (this is shown in the following image).

  Cancer classification and prediction has become one of the most important applications of DNA microarray due to their capabilities in cancer diagnostic and prognostic predictions.

- **Multinomial logistic regression**: Problems with more than two categories are referred to as multinomial logistic regressions.

  Insurance risk classification is an example of multinomial logistic regression.

  Risk classification (high risk, medium risk, and low risk) is an important part of the actuarial process in insurance companies. It helps set fair premiums and it is capable of classifying the clients according to their behavioral patterns.

  Furthermore, credit risk analysis (credit models) is used to evaluate the risk of consumer loans, evaluate loan applicants, and credit scoring based on historical and existing client bank transactions.

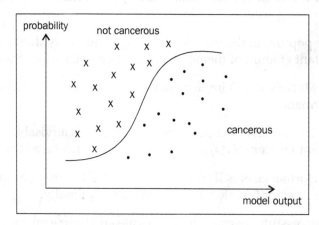

A real-world example

We can use logistic regression to predict whether a patient has a given disease, based on the available symptoms and other circumstances, such as age and heredity.

In this example, we will see how we can predict whether the patient has a risk of having cancer (breast cancer, for example) based on their gene information.

Gene selection is performed with thousands of genes (shown in the next image) to find potential cancer-causing genes.

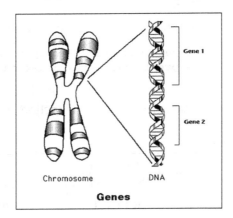

The following is a sample dataset that we will be using in our example; this should be available in the .csv format (for example, save the following table as gene.csv):

gene1	gene2	gene3	gene4	Has cancer?
1	0	1	0	1
1	0	1	0	1
1	1	1	1	0
1	1	1	1	0
0	1	1	1	0

The logistic function for the preceding scenario is shown in the following image:

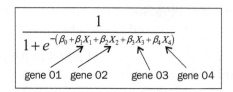

An example script

The following is the Mahout command for the logistic regression algorithm:

```
./mahout  trainlogistic --input "gene.csv" --output ./model --target
HasCancer --categories 2  --predictors gene1 gene2 gene3 gene4  --types
numeric --features 4
```

The important parameters for the `trainlogistic` function are explained in the following table:

Parameter name	Description
input	This is the input dataset (file resource)
output	The model is saved as the name given here
target	This is the target variable field
categories	This refers to the number of categories or labels
predictors	These are the predictor variable fields
types	This is the list of types of the predictor variables (numeric, word, and text)
features	This is the number of features

The outcome of the execution of the `trainlogistic` method is shown in the following image:

```
4
HasCancer ~
0.000*Intercept Term + 0.001*gene1 + 0.001*gene2 + 0.001*gene3 + 0.001*gene4
    Intercept Term 0.00016
             gene1 0.00146
             gene2 0.00146
             gene3 0.00146
             gene4 0.00146
     0.000000000      0.000155400      0.001463619      0.000000000
```

Testing and evaluation

Now, let's evaluate the model generated using the same dataset, using the following command:

```
./mahout runlogistic --input "gene.csv" --model ./model --auc -confusion
```

The following image shows the output result of the `runlogistic` method:

```
AUC = 1.00
confusion: [[0.0, 0.0], [2.0, 3.0]]
```

There are several methods to access the accuracy of the model.

The confusion matrix

A confusion matrix (shown in the following image) is a table that is used to describe the performance of a classification model on a set of test data for which the true values are known.

	p' (Predicted)	n' (Predicted)
p (Actual)	True Positive	False Negative
n (Actual)	False Positive	True Negative

The area under the curve

Accuracy is measured by the area under the **Receiver Operating Characteristic (ROC)** curve measure.

A perfect model will achieve a true positive rate of 1 and a false positive rate of 0.

A perfect model will score an **Area Under the Curve (AUC)** of 1, while random guessing will score an AUC of around 0.5. In practice, all models will fit somewhere in between.

The Naïve Bayes algorithm

The Naïve Bayes is a probabilistic classifier based on Bayes' theorem. This assumes strong (naive) independence assumptions between the features.

As long as features are not correlated and not repetitive, both Naïve Bayes and logistic regression will perform in a similar manner. However, when features are correlated and repetitive, the Naïve Bayes algorithm behaves differently due to its conditional independence assumption.

The Bayes theorem

This is the mathematical equation for the Bayes theorem:

$$P(A \mid B) = \frac{P(B \mid A) P(A)}{P(B)}$$

Bayes theorem

Here, A and B are events:

- P(A) and P(B) are the probabilities of A and B, independent of each other
- P(A | B), a conditional probability, is the probability of A given that B is true
- P(B | A), is the probability of B given that A is true

Text classification

Text classification is the task of classifying documents by their content (by the words that they contain). The best-known current text classification problem is e-mail spam filtering.

Did you know?

Spam filtering using text classification

Naive Bayes classifiers are a popular statistical technique of e-mail filtering. They typically use bag-of-words features to identify spam e-mails, an approach that is commonly used in text classification.

- By volume, spam filtering is easily the biggest application of text classification

- Extract features from the header and content

- Misspellings, character set choice, and HTML games mislead the extraction of words

- It also puts content in to images

- Forge headers (in order avoid identification but also interfere with classification)

An example spam e-mail is shown in the following image:

```
📧 googleteam                          GOOGLE LOTTERY WINNER!

From: googleteam  To:
Subject: GOOGLE LOTTERY WINNER! CONTACT YOUR AGENT TO CLAIM YOUR PRIZE.

GOOGLE  LOTTERY INTERNATIONAL
INTERNATIONAL PROMOTION / PRIZE AWARD .
(WE ENCOURAGE GLOBALI7ATION)
FROM: THE LOTTERY COORDINATOR,
GOOGLE B.V. 44 9459 PE.
RESULTS FOR CATEGORY "A" DRAWS

Congratulations to you as we bring to your notice the results of
the first Grand Summer Lottery. We are glad to announce that
your email ID has emerged as the winner of $1,000,000.
Congrats once again.
Your fund is now deposited with the paying bank. In your interest
of getting the amount early, you are requested to pay a nominal
processing amount to the bank. Details are attached with this mail.
```

Naïve assumption and its pros and cons in text classification

Naive Bayes is fast and easy to implement. However, individual words in a textual content are not independent of each other in a realistic scenario.

Accordingly, even though the Naïve assumption in the Naïve Bayes algorithm enables efficiency in processing, it adversely affects the quality or accuracy of results.

Improvements that Apache Mahout has made to the Naïve Bayes classification

Apache Mahout has provided simple heuristic solutions to address the problems, as follows:

1. Multinomial Naive Bayes does not model text well in terms of handling word occurrence dependencies.
2. When one class has more training examples than another, Naive Bayes selects poor weights for the decision boundary (the bias effect) or the problem of uneven training data.

A text classification coding example using the 20 newsgroups' example

Let's take a look at an example with 20 newsgroups.

Understand the 20 newsgroups' dataset

The 20 newsgroups collection has been used in many experiments related to text classification. This has around 20,000 documents that belong to 20 newsgroups.

The following screenshot shows the organization of the newsgroups (categories):

The 20 newsgroups dataset consists of messages, one per file. Here's one such message:

```
○ ○ ○                         103117
From: manes@magpie.linknet.com (Steve Manes)
Subject: Re: Oops! Oh no!
Organization: Manes and Associates, NYC
X-Newsreader: TIN [version 1.1 PL9]
Lines: 53

Wm. L. Ranck (ranck@joesbar.cc.vt.edu) wrote:
:    I hate to admit this, and I'm still mentally kicking myself for it.
: I rode the brand new K75RT home last Friday night.  100 miles in rain
: and darkness.  No problems.  Got it home and put it on the center stand.
:    The next day I pushed it off the center stand in preparation for going
: over to a friend's house to pose.  You guessed it.  It got away from me
: and landed on its right side.
:    Scratched the lower fairing, cracked the right mirror, and cracked the
: upper fairing.
:    *DAMN* am I stupid!  It's going to cost me ~$200 to get the local
: body shop to fix it.  And that is after I take the fairing off for them.
: Still, that's probably cheaper than the mirror alone if I bought a
: replacement from BMW.
```

Execute the complete example script using the following commands:

```
cd MAHOUT_HOME/examples/bin/
./classify-20newsgroups.sh
```

Text classification using Naïve Bayes – a MapReduce implementation with Hadoop

The instructions for setting up Hadoop are given in *Chapter 5, Apache Mahout in Production*, of this book.

1. Set the HADOOP_HOME variable to the Hadoop installation folder:

   ```
   HADOOP_HOME="/home/jayani/hadoop-2.6.0"
   ```

2. Set the Hadoop configuration paths:

   ```
   HADOOP_CONF_DIR="/home/jayani/hadoop-2.6.0/etc/hadoop"
   ```

   You can add MAHOUT_HOME/bin as the PATH variable for ease of use, as follows:

   ```
   export PATH=$PATH:/home/jayani/mahout_home/bin
   ```

3. Copy data to HDFS using Hadoop's dfs put command.

4. Create sequence files:

   ```
   mahout seqdirectory -i 20news-all -o 20news-seq -ow
   ```

The following image shows the generated sequence files:

```
-rw-r--r--   2 hduser supergroup          0 2015-03-24 07:54 20news-seq/_SUCCESS
-rw-r--r--   2 hduser supergroup   19202391 2015-03-24 07:54 20news-seq/part-m-00000
```

You can display the content in the sequence file using the following command:

```
hdfs dfs -text 20news-seq/part-m-00000
```

An example key, value pair is shown in the following screenshot:

```
/talk.religion.misc/84357        From: alizard@tweekco.uucp (A.Lizard)
Subject: Re: 14 Apr 93   God's Promise in 1 John 1: 7
Organization: Tweek-Com Systems BBS, Moraga, CA (510) 631-0615
Lines: 20

starowl@rahul.net (Michael D. Adams) writes:
> : If anyone in .netland is in the process of devising a new religion,
> : do not use the lamb or the bull, because they have already been
> : reserved.  Please choose another animal, preferably one not
> : on the Endangered Species List.
>
> How about "washed in the blood of Barney the Dinosaur"?  :)

Judging from postings I've read all over Usenet and on non-Usenet
BBs conferences, Barney is DEFINITELY an endangered species. Especially
if he runs into me in a dark alley.

                              A.Lizard

----------------------------------------------------------------------
A.Lizard Internet Addresses:
alizard%tweekco%boo@PacBell.COM        (preferred)
PacBell.COM!boo!tweekco!alizard (bang path for above)
alizard@gentoo.com (backup)
PGP2.2 public key available on request

/talk.religion.misc/84358        From: alizard@tweekco.uucp (A.Lizard)
Subject: Re: OTO, the Ancient Order of Oriental Templars
Organization: Tweek-Com Systems BBS, Moraga, CA (510) 631-0615
Lines: 18

Thyagi@cup.portal.com (Thyagi Morgoth NagaSiva) writes:

> "This organization is known at the present time as the Ancient
> Order of Oriental Templars.  Ordo Templi Orientis.  Otherwise:
> The Hermetic Brotherhood of Light.
>
Does this organization have an official e-mail address these
days? (an address for any of the SF Bay Area Lodges, e.g. Thelema
would do.)
                              93...
                              A.Lizard

----------------------------------------------------------------------
A.Lizard Internet Addresses:
alizard%tweekco%boo@PacBell.COM        (preferred)
PacBell.COM!boo!tweekco!alizard (bang path for above)
alizard@gentoo.com (backup)
PGP2.2 public key available on request
```

1. Convert sequence files to vectors:

   ```
   mahout seq2sparse -i 20news-seq -o 20news-vectors  -lnorm -nv  -wt
   tfidf
   ```

   The files generated from the preceding step are shown in the following screenshot:

```
drwxr-xr-x   - hduser supergroup          0 2015-03-26 11:13 20news-vectors/df-count
-rw-r--r--   2 hduser supergroup    1937084 2015-03-26 11:12 20news-vectors/dictionary.file-0
-rw-r--r--   2 hduser supergroup    1890053 2015-03-26 11:13 20news-vectors/frequency.file-0
drwxr-xr-x   - hduser supergroup          0 2015-03-26 11:14 20news-vectors/tf-vectors
drwxr-xr-x   - hduser supergroup          0 2015-03-26 11:15 20news-vectors/tfidf-vectors
drwxr-xr-x   - hduser supergroup          0 2015-03-26 11:11 20news-vectors/tokenized-documents
drwxr-xr-x   - hduser supergroup          0 2015-03-26 11:12 20news-vectors/wordcount
```

2. Split the training and test datasets:

```
mahout split -i 20news-vectors/tfidf-vectors --trainingOutput
20news-train-vectors --testOutput 20news-test-vectors
--randomSelectionPct 40 --overwrite --sequenceFiles -xm sequential
```

3. Train using the Naïve Bayes algorithm:

```
mahout trainnb -i 20news-train-vectors -el -o model -li labelindex
-ow
```

4. Test the generated model:

```
mahout testnb -i 20news-test-vectors -m model -l labelindex -ow -o
20news-testing
```

The output of the preceding step is shown in the following screenshot:

```
===================================================================
Statistics
-------------------------------------------------------------------
Kappa                                            0.8721
Accuracy                                         90.1208%
Reliability                                      85.4905%
Reliability (standard deviation)                 0.2164
Weighted precision                               0.9061
Weighted recall                                  0.9012
Weighted F1 score                                0.9002
15/02/10 14:38:17 INFO test.TestNaiveBayesDriver: Standard NB Results:
===================================================================
Summary
-------------------------------------------------------------------
Correctly Classified Instances       :    6641      90.1208%
Incorrectly Classified Instances     :     728       9.8792%
Total Classified Instances           :    7369
===================================================================
```

The different measures mentioned in the outcome to evaluate the model are mentioned here:

- **Kappa statistics**: The Kappa statistic is a metric that compares an observed accuracy with an expected accuracy
- **Reliability**: This is the extent to which a measurement gives results that are consistent
- **Precision**: This is the fraction of retrieved instances that are relevant
- **Recall**: This is the fraction of relevant instances that are retrieved
- **F1 measure**: This is a measure that combines precision and recall

Further, you can display the label index using the following command:

```
mahout seqdumper -i labelindex
```

The label index displayed using the preceding command is shown in the following screenshot:

```
Input Path: labelindex
Key class: class org.apache.hadoop.io.Text Value Class: class org.apache.hadoop.io.IntWritable
Key: alt.atheism: Value: 0
Key: comp.graphics: Value: 1
Key: comp.os.ms-windows.misc: Value: 2
Key: comp.sys.ibm.pc.hardware: Value: 3
Key: comp.sys.mac.hardware: Value: 4
Key: comp.windows.x: Value: 5
Key: misc.forsale: Value: 6
Key: rec.autos: Value: 7
Key: rec.motorcycles: Value: 8
Key: rec.sport.baseball: Value: 9
Key: rec.sport.hockey: Value: 10
Key: sci.crypt: Value: 11
Key: sci.electronics: Value: 12
Key: sci.med: Value: 13
Key: sci.space: Value: 14
Key: soc.religion.christian: Value: 15
Key: talk.politics.guns: Value: 16
Key: talk.politics.mideast: Value: 17
Key: talk.politics.misc: Value: 18
Key: talk.religion.misc: Value: 19
Count: 20
```

You can use the `vectordumper` command to display the content of TF-IDF vectors:

```
mahout vectordump -i 20news-vectors/tfidf-vectors
```

Text classification using Naïve Bayes – the Spark implementation

We have mentioned how to set up Spark in detail in the previous section (using linear regression). Here are the steps that you need to perform in order to set up Spark:

1. Set the SPARK_HOME path.
2. Start the Spark server.
3. Train the dataset and generate the model:

   ```
   mahout spark-trainnb -i 20news-train-vectors -el -o model -li
   labelindex -ow
   ```

4. Test and evaluate the dataset:

   ```
   mahout spark-testnb -i 20news-train-vectors -m model -l labelindex
   -ow -o 20news-testing
   ```

Apache Mahout contains an example script, which includes all the steps in one go in the following path.

It contains several classification algorithms such as CNaiveBayes, Naïve Bayes, and SGD.

To execute the script, use the following command:

```
MAHOUT_HOME/examples/bin/classify-20newsgroups.sh
```

The Markov chain

The Markov chain is a finite state machine with probabilistic state transitions.

It is a probabilistic method that depends on the current state to predict the next state. For the Markov chain to be successful, the current state has to be dependent on the previous state in some way.

It makes the Markov assumption that the next state only depends on the current state and is independent of previous history.

Hidden Markov Model

A **Hidden Markov Model (HMM)** is a statistical Markov model in which the system being modeled is assumed to be a Markov process with unobserved (hidden) states.

HMM is a generative probabilistic model. HMM is used with data that is represented as a series of states from a series of observations. The transitions between hidden states are assumed to have the form of a (first-order) Markov chain.

HMM is mostly applied in temporal pattern recognition problems.

A real-world example – developing a POS tagger using HMM supervised learning

To demonstrate the HMM algorithm, let's take **Part Of Speech (POS)** tagging as an example.

POS tagging

POS tagging is important for many **Natural Language Processing (NLP)** tasks, such as word sense disambiguation, syntax parsing, machine language translation, and **Named Entity Recognition (NER)**. In POS tagging, we identify words as part of speech, such as nouns, verbs, adjectives, and adverbs.

This is a key step in the lowest level of syntactical analysis.

POS tagging can be done using rule-based methods and learning-based methods. However, learning-based approaches have been found to be more effective.

The following image contains an example sentence with POS tags:

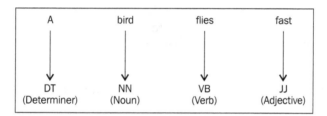

Annotating a sequence of words with their POS tags:

- Input: A bird flies fast
- Output: A (DT) bird (NN) flies (VB) fast (JJ)

HMM for POS tagging

In HMM, POS tagging is considered to be a sequence labeling problem. The sequence of tags is viewed as a Markov chain.

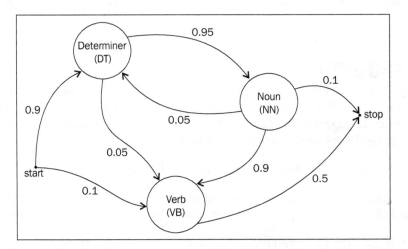

As shown in the previous image, we make the assumption that a word's tag only depends on the previous tag. We don't get to observe the actual sequence of states (POS tags). Somewhat, we can only observe some of the outcome generated by each state (words).

Before moving onto the code examples, let's understand some important concepts about HMMs, as follows:

- **Hidden states**: Hidden states are unobserved states. In POS tagging content, hidden states are POS tags for each word.

- **Observed states**: Observed states are the output or are dependent on the hidden state. In POS tagging, words form the output.

- **Transition matrix**: All the possible transition probabilities from one hidden state to the next hidden state are represented in the transition matrix. For example, in POS tagging, the transition matrix consists of the probabilities of the next POS tag given the previous POS tag.

- **Emission matrix**: The probabilities of observed states that are given a hidden state are represented in an emission matrix. In POS tagging, the emission probability is the probabilities of the possible observed states (**words**), given a hidden state (a POS tag).

The preceding concepts are represented in the following image of a POS-tagging scenario:

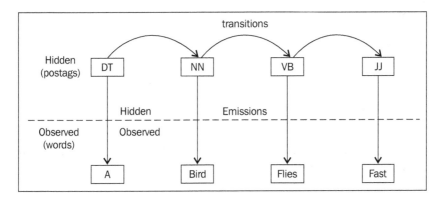

HMM implementation in Apache Mahout

Apache Mahout has different implementations of the HMM algorithm, as follows:

- Training
    - ○ Supervised

        HMM

    - ○ Unsupervised

        Viterbi training

        Baum Welch training

- Evaluation
    - ○ Viterbi decoding
    - ○ Forward/backward (compute likelihood)

HMM supervised learning

Apache Mahout contains an example on POS tagging using the supervised HMM algorithm as given as follows under Mahout examples:

- **Package**: org.apache.mahout.classifier.sequencelearning.hmm
- **Class**: POStagger.java

Code example:

1. Train the model:

```
HmmModel
org.apache.mahout.classifier.sequencelearning.hmm.HmmTrainer.train
SupervisedSequence(int nrOfHiddenStates, int nrOfOutputStates,
Collection<int[]> hiddenSequences, Collection<int[]>
observedSequences, double pseudoCount)
```

Create a supervised initial estimate of an HMM model based on a number of sequences of observed and hidden states.

The important parameters

Important parameters for HMM supervised learning algorithm is given in the following table:

Parameter name	Description
nrOfHiddenStates	The total number of hidden states
nrOfOutputStates	The total number of output states
hiddenSequences	A collection of hidden sequences to use for training (tags are given an ID)
observedSequences	A collection of the observed sequences to use for training, associated with hidden sequences (words are given an ID)
pseudoCount	The value that is assigned to nonoccurring transitions in order to avoid zero probabilities

Returns

An initial model using the estimated parameters (HmmModel).

Test the model using HMMEvaluator.

The `HMMEvaluator` class offers several methods to evaluate a HMM model.

The following use cases are covered:

1. Generate a sequence of output states from a given model (prediction).
2. Compute the likelihood that a given model generated a given sequence of output states (a model likelihood).
3. Compute the most likely hidden sequence for a given model and a given observed sequence (decoding) using the Viterbi algorithm.

The following screenshot contains the console output of the HMM POS tagging example:

```
15/02/04 18:50:46 INFO hmm.PosTagger: McDonalds[NNP]
15/02/04 18:50:46 INFO hmm.PosTagger: is[VBZ]
15/02/04 18:50:46 INFO hmm.PosTagger: a[DT]
15/02/04 18:50:46 INFO hmm.PosTagger: huge[JJ]
15/02/04 18:50:46 INFO hmm.PosTagger: company[NN]
15/02/04 18:50:46 INFO hmm.PosTagger: with[IN]
15/02/04 18:50:46 INFO hmm.PosTagger: many[JJ]
15/02/04 18:50:46 INFO hmm.PosTagger: employees[NNS]
15/02/04 18:50:46 INFO hmm.PosTagger: .[.]
```

The Baum Welch algorithm

The Baum Welch algorithm is an unsupervised learning mechanism. It is used to estimate the parameters of the model. This sets the emission probability and transmission probabilities using the iterative expectation maximization algorithm.

When given only the observed states of the model, the Baum Welch algorithm gives the following outcomes:

- Most likely hidden transition probabilities
- Most likely set of emission probabilities

A code example

1. Prepare the input data:

```
echo "0 1 2 2 2 1 1 0 0 3 3 3 2 1 2 1 1 1 1 2 2 2 0 0 0 0 0 0 2 2
2 0 0 0 0 0 2 2 2 3 3 3 3 3 3 2 3 2 3 2 3 2 1 3 0 0 0 1 0 1 0 2
1 2 1 2 1 2 3 3 3 3 2 2 3 2 1 1 0" > hmm-input
```

2. Train the model:

```
$ export MAHOUT_LOCAL=true
```

> $ $MAHOUT_HOME/bin/mahout baumwelch -i hmm-input -o
> hmm-model -nh 3 -no 4 -e .0001 -m 1000

The important parameters

Important parameters for Baum-Welch algorithm is given in the following table:

Parameter name	Description
-i	Input
-o	Output
-nh	The number of hidden states
-no	The number of observed states
-e	The convergence threshold
-m	Maximum number of iterations

The following screenshot shows the output of the training algorithm:

```
Initial probabilities:
0 1 2
1.222781817993575E-39 1.0 0.0
Transition matrix:
   0 1 2
0 0.19657722835122673 0.8034220477016764 7.239470969040812E-7
1 0.8590970274728559 1.9794577861051145E-6 0.14090099306935794
2 6.408978671067206E-14 0.1306968267864915 0.8693031732134443
Emission matrix:
   0 1 2 3
0 0.38974684679808286 0.439249333191133336 0.17100382129058372 5.311403977947581E-33
1 0.4070125431910323 0.11628999131607592 0.4766974654928918 1.9607767417392144E-18
2 2.0301873727746794E-65 0.042979838315800586 0.29677015848116833 0.660250003203031
```

The Viterbi evaluator

Once you have trained HMM using any of the preceding methods, use the Viterbi decoding algorithm to compute the most likely sequence of states, which may have generated your observations.

The transition probabilities for the hidden part of your model and the emission probabilities for the visible outputs of your model have to be known in order to apply Viterbi evaluation on the data.

This is used in the `HMMEvaluator.java` class for model evaluation purposes.

- **Project**: `Mahout-core`
- **Package**: `org.apache.mahout.classifier.sequencelearning.hmm`
- **Class**: `HMMEvaluator.java`

In the POS scenario, this refers to tagging each token (word) in a sequence with a label (a POS tag).

In a POS scenario, we now turn to the problem of finding the most likely tag sequence for an input sentence.

The Apache Mahout references

- (HMM Baum Welch): `https://mahout.apache.org/users/classification/hidden-markov-models.html`

Summary

In this chapter we learned that classification and regression are supervised learning problems, which require labeled data. Predictor variables and output variables should be defined to come up with a model during the training phase.

We also saw that supervised learning can be achieved using different techniques, namely model-based, regression-based and tree-based techniques.

Regression can be divided into two categories based on the outcome of the algorithm, that is linear regression and logistic regression.

We saw that text classification is an important application and this is explained using the Naïve Bayes algorithm.

In the next chapter, we will discuss the recommendation techniques using Apache Mahout.

4
Recommendations

In this chapter, we will cover the recommendation techniques used in Apache Mahout. We will discuss the related MapReduce- and Spark-based implementations with respect to a real-world example, with Java code examples as well as command-line executions.

In this chapter, we will cover the following topics:

- Collaborative versus content-based filtering
- User-based recommenders
- Data models
- Similarity
- Neighborhoods
- Recommenders
- Item-based recommenders with Spark
- Matrix factorization-based recommenders
    - SVD recommenders
    - ALS-WS
- Evaluation techniques
- Recommendation tips and tricks

"A lot of times, people don't know what they want until you show it to them."

– Steve Jobs

Before we proceed with the chapter, let's think about the significance of the preceding quote for a moment.

- How many times have you come across relevant items to buy, which were suggested by Amazon recommendations?
- How many times have you found your friends when suggested by Facebook, which you did not notice earlier?
- How many videos have you watched when recommended by YouTube, which you ultimately found to be useful later?

The volume of available information is growing at an alarming rate.

By 2014, Facebook had around 1.35 billion active users. The number of electronic items itself is around 24 million in Amazon. There are approximately 9,796 movies on Netflix.

Consequently, filtering out relevant information is essential to make the right decisions and realize new information.

Collaborative versus content-based filtering

There are two main approaches you can take when it comes to filtering information.

Content-based filtering

Content-based filtering is an unsupervised mechanism based on the attributes of the items and the preferences and model of the user.

For example, if a user views a movie with a certain set of attributes, such as genre, actors, and awards, the systems recommend items with similar attributes. The preferences of the user (for example, previous "likes" for movies) are mapped with the attributes or features of the recommended item.

User ratings are not required in this approach. However, this approach requires considerable effort when it comes to feature or attribute extraction, and it is also relatively less precise than collaborative filtering approaches, which we will discuss later.

Collaborative filtering

Collaborative filtering approaches consider the notion of similarity between items and users. The features of a product or the properties of users are not considered here, as in content-based filtering.

As shown in the following image, you must be familiar with statements such as "people who bought this item also bought.." and "people who viewed this item also viewed...," which represent the collaborative filtering approach in real-world applications.

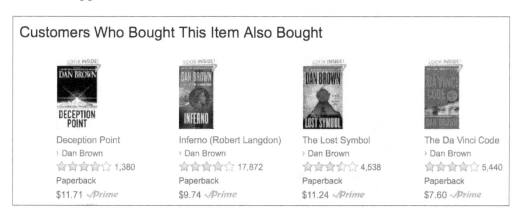

In collaborative filtering, for each item or user, a neighborhood is formed with similar related items or users. Once you view an item, recommendations are drawn from that neighborhood.

The collaborative filtering approach uses historical data on user behavior, such as clicks, views, and purchases, to provide better recommendations.

Collaborative filtering can be achieved using the following techniques.

- Item-based recommendations
- User-based recommendations
- Matrix factorization-based recommendations

Apache Mahout has implemented machine learning algorithms to enable collaborative filtering approaches. So, in this chapter, we will mainly discuss this approach as opposed to content-based approaches.

Hybrid filtering

If both content-based and collaborative filtering approaches are used at the same time to provide recommendations, then the approach is known as hybrid filtering.

User-based recommenders

In user-based recommenders, similar users from a given neighborhood are identified and item recommendations are given based on what similar users already bought or viewed, which a particular user did not buy or view yet.

For example, as shown in the following figure, if **Nimal** likes the movies **Interstellar (2014)** and **Lucy (2014)** and **Sunil** also likes the same movies, and in addition, if **Sunil** likes **The Matrix (1999)** as well, then we can recommend **The Matrix (1999)** to **Nimal**, as the chances are that **Nimal** and **Sunil** are like-minded people.

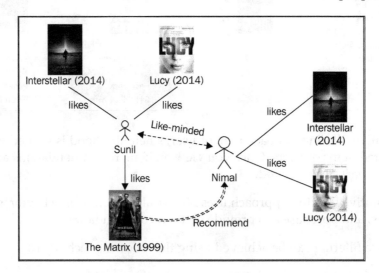

A real-world example – movie recommendations

Let's explain this approach using a real-world example on a movie recommendation site, as shown in the following figure:

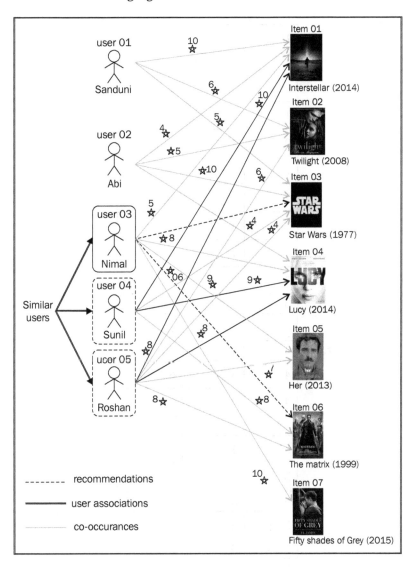

Users who watched the movies (items) rated them according to their preferences. The rating is a value between 1 (lowest) and 10 (highest).

The user, item, and preferences (ratings) information is given in the following table; you need to save this data as `movies.csv` in order to execute the example that follows:

User	Item	Rating
1	1	10
1	2	6
1	3	5
2	1	4
2	2	5
2	3	10
2	4	4
3	1	5
3	4	8
3	5	9
3	7	10
4	1	10
4	3	6
4	4	9
4	6	8
5	1	8
5	2	6
5	3	4
5	4	8
5	5	7
5	6	8

The Java code example for user-based recommendations is given as follows:

```
DataModel model = new FileDataModel (new File("movie.csv"));

UserSimilarity similarity = new PearsonCorrelationSimilarity (model);

UserNeighborhood neighborhood = new NearestNUserNeighborhood (2,
similarity, model);

Recommender recommender = new GenericUserBasedRecommender (model,
neighborhood, similarity);

List<RecommendedItem> recommendations = recommender.recommend(3, 2);

for (RecommendedItem recommendation : recommendations) {
  System.out.println(recommendation);
}
```

In this example, we need to get the top two recommendations for **user 03** (**Nimal**). User 03 liked the following movies, with the given ratings in brackets:

```
User 3 > Item 1 (5), Item 4 (8), Item 5 (9), Item 7 (10)
```

Here, we can see that **user 04** and **user 05** share some similar interests (**Item 01** and **Item 04**) with **user 03**. So, we assume that **user 03** might like the other items that **user 04** and **user 05** likes, which **user 03** has not tried out before. Accordingly, we recommend **Item 06** and **Item 03**.

```
User 4 > Item 1, Item 4, Item 6 (8), Item 3 (6)
User 5 > Item 1, Item 2, Item 3 (4), Item 4, Item 5, Item 6 (8)
```

This shows the result of the code example:

```
RecommendedItem[item:6, value:8.0]
RecommendedItem[item:3, value:5.181073]
```

The value of `item:6` is higher than that of `item:3` because both `User 4` and `User 5` have rated `item:6` higher.

Even though **user 01** and **user 02** have some common interests (**Item 01** and **Item 04**) with **user 03**, they are not considered due to low ratings given to these co-occurring items.

When we walk-through this code, we learn a few significant abstractions that have been provided by Apache Mahout.

Data models

A data model represents how we read data from different data sources. In our code example, we used `FileDataModel`, which takes **comma-separated values (CSV)** as input.

In addition, Apache Mahout supports the following input methods:

- `JDBCDataModel`: This method reads from the JDBC driver

- `GenericDataModel`: This is populated through Java calls

- `GenericBooleanPrefDataModel`: This uses the given user data, which is suitable for small experiments

The following is the code example with `GenericDataModel`:

```
// Preferences for all users
FastByIDMap<PreferenceArray> userData=new
FastByIDMap<PreferenceArray>();

// Preferences for user 1
List<Preference> prefsUser1=new ArrayList<Preference>();
prefsUser1.add(new GenericPreference(1,1,10));
prefsUser1.add(new GenericPreference(1,4,9));

// Preferences for user 2
List<Preference> prefsUser2=new ArrayList<Preference>();
prefsUser2.add(new GenericPreference(2,1,10));

// Preferences for user 3
List<Preference> prefsUser3=new ArrayList<Preference>();
prefsUser3.add(new GenericPreference(3,1,10));
prefsUser3.add(new GenericPreference(3,2,8));
prefsUser3.add(new GenericPreference(3,3,5));

// Add preferences for all users
userData.put(1,new GenericUserPreferenceArray(prefsUser1));
userData.put(2,new GenericUserPreferenceArray(prefsUser2));
userData.put(3,new GenericUserPreferenceArray(prefsUser3));

DataModel model = new GenericDataModel(userData);
// Get possible unseen preferred items for user 2
CandidateItemsStrategy strategy=new
SamplingCandidateItemsStrategy(1,1);
FastIDSet candidateItems=strategy.getCandidateItems(2,new
GenericUserPreferenceArray(prefsUser2),model);
```

```
for (Long candidateRecommendation : candidateItems) {
  System.out.println("Candidate item: " +
  candidateRecommendation);
}
```

The `userData` variable contains preferences of all the users for the items available along with their ratings. `PreferenceArray` is a memory-efficient way of having a collection of preferences for each user. `Preference` contains a user's preference for an item with the preference value (rating). You can filter out the considered items and users for result candidate items using `CandidateItemStrategy`.

The result for the preceding code example is given as follows:

```
Candidate item: 2
Candidate item: 3
Candidate item: 4
```

As you can see from the result, items 2, 3, and 4 are recommended for `user 2`, as these are the items that `user 2` has not rated but users with similar preferences to `user 2` (`user 1` and `user 2`) have rated.

The similarity measure

Similarity represents the similarity between two users in user-based recommendations or the similarity between two items in item-based recommendations.

Two users can be considered to be similar if the distance or angle between them is small in the user – item space. An example of this is shown in the following figure:

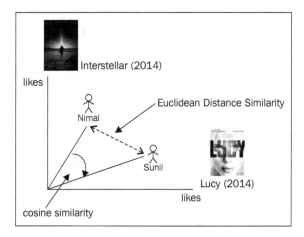

In our example, we have used the `PearsonCorrelationSimilarity` measure to find similarity between two users. Some other available similarity measures are listed as follows:

- `EuclideanDistanceSimilarity`: This measures the Euclidean distance between two users or items as dimensions and preference values given will be values along those dimensions. `EuclideanDistanceSimilarity` will not work if you have not given preference values.

- `TanimotoCoefficientSimilarity`: This is applicable if preference values consist of binary responses (`true` and `false`). `TanimotoCoefficientSimilarity` is the number of similar items two users bought or the total number of items they bought.

- `LogLikelihoodSimilarity`: This is a measure based on likelihood ratios. The number of co-occurring events, in this context, the number of times either users or items that occurred together and the number of times either users or items that do not occur together, are considered for evaluating similarity.

- `SpearmanCorrelationSimilarity`: In `SpearmanCorrelationSimilarity`, the relative rankings of preference values are compared instead of preference values.

- `UncenteredCosineSimilarity`: This is an implementation of cosine similarity. The angle between two preference vectors is considered for calculation.

When defining similarity measures, you need to keep in mind that not all datasets will work with all similarity measures. You need to consider the nature of the dataset when selecting a similarity measure.

Also, to determine the optimal similarity measure for your scenario, you need to have a good understanding of the dataset.

Trying out different similarity measures with your training dataset is essential to find the optimal similarity measure.

The neighborhood

Using the selected neighborhood algorithm, we can compute the "neighborhood" of users for a given user. This neighborhood can be used to compute recommendations.

An example of a movie recommendation scenario is given in the following figure:

We have used the nearest neighbour algorithm in the preceding example.

- **Nearest neighbour algorithm**: This calculates a neighborhood comprising of the nearest N users to a given user

- **ThresholdUserNeighborhood**: This calculates a neighborhood comprising of all the users whose similarity to the given user is the same as or outstrips a given threshold

Recommenders

Given the data model neighborhood and similarity, the selected Apache Mahout recommender estimates similar items for unseen or new items for the user.

Different recommenders such as `GenericUserBasedRecommender`, `GenericItemBasedRecommender`, and `SVDRecommender` are explained in this chapter in detail.

Evaluation techniques

A good recommender should be able to infer the items that users are likely to be interested in.

There are two different methods to evaluate the quality of a recommender for a given dataset, as follows:

- Prediction-based
- Information Retrieval (IR-based)

During the evaluation, the dataset is split into training and test datasets. The training dataset is used to create the model, and evaluation is done based on the test dataset. In the following example, 0.8 is given as the evaluation percentage.

The IR-based method (precision/recall)

The code example to evaluate the recommender with the IR-based method is given here.

In the recommendation context, Precision denotes the fraction of top recommendations that are relevant recommendations. Recall denotes the fraction of relevant recommendations that appear in the top recommendations:

```
DataModel model = new FileDataModel (new File("movie.csv"));

RecommenderIRStatsEvaluator evaluator = new
GenericRecommenderIRStatsEvaluator();
RecommenderBuilder builder = new RecommenderBuilder() {
  public Recommender buildRecommender(DataModel model) throws
  TasteException {
    UserSimilarity similarity = new
    LogLikelihoodSimilarity(model);
    UserNeighborhood neighborhood = new
    NearestNUserNeighborhood(5, similarity, model);
    return new GenericUserBasedRecommender(model, neighborhood,
    similarity);
  }
};

IRStatistics stats = evaluator.evaluate(builder, null, model,
null, 2, GenericRecommenderIRStatsEvaluator.CHOOSE_THRESHOLD,
0.8);
System.out.println("Precision: " + stats.getPrecision()+" Recall:
" + stats.getRecall());
}
```

Addressing the issues with inaccurate recommendation results

The accuracy of the recommendation results mainly relies on finding the right similarity measure and the right neighborhood algorithm that fits the dataset in hand well.

If the dataset is sparse (if there are large number of items and less number of user preferences), `PearsonCorrelationSimilarity` will provide a better solution than `UncenteredCosineSimilarity`.

The nearest neighbor graph and the distance similarity distribution can be used to examine the similarity measure further.

Distance distribution is based on measures such as average neighbor similarity, neighbor similarity ratio, and neighbor stability, whereas the nearest neighbor graph is based on average graph distance, clustering coefficient, graph density, graph diameter, and maximum graph distance.

Moreover, a threshold can be used to filter out the inaccurate results. If values are missing, we can introduce some default values or eliminate that data.

Item-based recommenders

An item-based recommender measures the similarities between different items and picks the top k closest (in similarity) items to a given item in order to arrive at a rating prediction or recommendation for a given user for a given item.

For the movie recommendation scenario, an item-based recommender works as given in the following figure:

Let's say both **Sunil** and **Roshan** like the movies **Interstellar (2014)** and **Star Wars (1977)**. Then, we can infer that **Interstellar (2014)** and **Star Wars (1977)** could be similar items. So, when **Nimal** likes **Interstellar (2014)**, we recommend **Star Wars (1977)** to **Nimal** based on our previous observation.

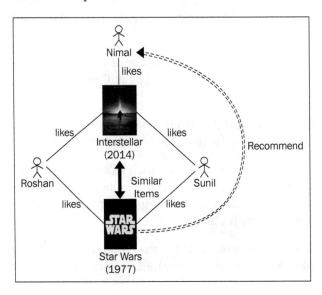

The following is the Java code example for item-based recommenders:

```java
DataModel model = new FileDataModel (new File("movie.csv"));

ItemSimilarity itemSimilarity = new EuclideanDistanceSimilarity
(model);

Recommender itemRecommender = new
GenericItemBasedRecommender(model,itemSimilarity);

List<RecommendedItem> itemRecommendations =
itemRecommender.recommend(3, 2);

for (RecommendedItem itemRecommendation : itemRecommendations) {
   System.out.println("Item: " + itemRecommendation);
}
```

In the preceding code example, we recommend two items for user 3. The result is given as follows:

```
Item: RecommendedItem[item:2, value:7.7220707]
Item: RecommendedItem[item:3, value:7.5602336
```

Item-based recommenders with Spark

An item-based recommender can also be executed on top of Spark. We have given the steps to set up the Spark server in *Chapter 3, Regression and Classification* in detail.

1. Start the Spark servers:

   ```
   [SPARK_HOME]/sbin/start-all
   ```

2. Prepare the input data (only the user ID and item ID, no preference values).

3. Copy the input data to HDFS.

4. Execute the following `mahout` command to generate recommendations for each item:

   ```
   mahout spark-itemsimilarity --input inputfile --output
   outputdirectory
   ```

`movie.csv` can be used as `inputfile`, or else you can give your own data file as well.

The generated indicator matrix is given in the following figure; this can be found in the `outputdirectory/indicator-matrix/` directory:

```
4    5:1.184939225613002 6:1.184939225613002 2:1.184939225613002 7:0.5053430784314124 3:0.5053430784314124
7    5:2.231435513142097 4:0.5053430784314124
5    7:2.231435513142097 3:2.231435513142097 4:1.184939225613002 6:0.13844293808390518 2:0.13844293808390518
6    4:1.184939225613002 3:1.184939225613002 5:0.13844293808390518 2:0.13844293808390518
2    3:2.231435513142097 4:1.184939225613002 5:0.13844293808390518 6:0.13844293808390518
3    5:2.231435513142097 2:2.231435513142097 6:1.184939225613002 4:0.5053430784314124
1
```

Similar items for each other item are given in the indicator matrix, with a similarity value according to the following format:

```
itemIDx    itemIDy:valuey itemIDz:valuez
```

Matrix factorization-based recommenders

So far, we have discussed two main collaborative filtering approaches, namely user-based and item-based recommenders.

Even though they are capable of providing users with relevant recommendations, a major challenge that these approaches face is the sparsity of large datasets. Not all users will provide ratings on all the available items. Also, new items and new users tend to lack sufficient historical data to predict good recommendations. This is known as the **cold start problem**.

Further, the requirement for scalable recommendation algorithms remains the same along with the requirement to perform well in sparse datasets.

Also, some users tend to have a bias toward ratings, and the previous approaches have not made an attempt to correct this bias. Also, hidden patterns between the features of available items and the features of users that lead to certain ratings are not exploited.

Matrix factorization is another way of doing collaborative filtering, which is intended to solve the previously mentioned problems.

Ratings can be induced by certain imperceptible factors, which are not straightforward for us to estimate, so we need to use mathematical techniques to do that for us.

For example, if a particular user has rated **The Matrix**, the influence factor to do this can be the "amount of sci-fi involved in the movie." If the same user has rated **Titanic**, then the influence factor can be the "amount of romance involved in the movie." So, using matrix factorization methods, we can recommend **Her** movie to that particular user by inferring these factors (latent factors).

The following figure denotes an example feature space of the preceding scenario. However, factors are not necessarily intuitively understandable by humans. The distance between each movie can be used to relate those movies.

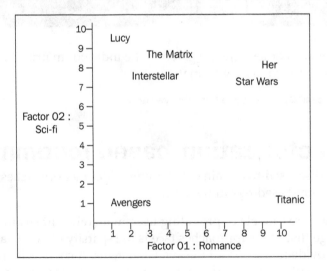

In Apache Mahout, there are a few methods on which matrix factorization can be done, as follows:

- Alternative Least Squares with Weighted-Lamda-Regularization (ALS-WS)
- SGD

SVD++ is a combination of matrix factorization and the latent factor model.

Alternative least squares

ALS-WS is one of the factorizers that can be used to generate recommendations, which is inherently parallel.

Mahout's ALS recommender is a matrix factorization algorithm that uses ALS-WR.

Singular value decomposition

Using **Singular Value Decomposition** (**SVD**), we can come up with a more generalized set of features to represent the user-item preferences for a large dataset using dimensionality reduction techniques. This approach helps to generalize users into lesser dimensions.

The following is the Java code example for SVD using ALS-WR as the factorizer; the number of target features should be given as input, which in this case (3. 0.065) is given as lambda (the regularization parameter), and the number of iterations is given as 1:

```
DataModel svdmodel = new FileDataModel (new File("movie.csv"));

ALSWRFactorizer factorizer = new ALSWRFactorizer(svdmodel, 3,
0.065, 1);

Recommender svdrecommender = new SVDRecommender(svdmodel, factorizer);
for (RecommendedItem recommendation :svdrecommender.recommend(3,1))
{
   System.out.println(recommendation);
}
```

The following is the output of the preceding code:

```
RecommendedItem[item:3, value:7.2046385]
```

The following is the command-line execution of the ALS-WS algorithm; the input and output directories should be available in HDFS:

```
mahout parallelALS --input alsmovieinput --output alsmovieoutput --lambda
0.1 --implicitFeedback true --alpha 0.8 --numFeatures 2 --numIterations 5
--numThreadsPerSolver 1 --tempDir tmp
```

In this approach, the user-to-item matrix is factored into the user-to-feature matrix (U) and the item-to-feature matrix (M), as shown in the following figure:

```
drwxr-xr-x   - jayani supergroup          0 2015-03-20 12:18 alsmovieoutput/M
drwxr-xr-x   - jayani supergroup          0 2015-03-20 12:18 alsmovieoutput/U
drwxr-xr-x   - jayani supergroup          0 2015-03-20 12:18 alsmovieoutput/userRatings
```

Then, we can get use the following command to get only the topmost recommendation for each item:

```
mahout recommendfactorized --input alsmovieinput --userFeatures
alsmovieoutput/U/ --itemFeatures alsmovieoutput/M/ --numRecommendations 1
--output recommendations --maxRating 1
```

The following figure shows the outcome of the preceding command:

```
1          [6:0.7240428]
2          [6:0.771763]
3          [6:0.34447142]
4          [2:0.8048554]
5          [7:0.16289039]
```

The resulting information can be embedded in a search engine, such as Apache Solr, to provide better search recommendations.

Algorithm usage tips and tricks

The optimal recommendation algorithm depends on the nature of data and the scenario in hand.

However, if you have fewer users than items, then it is better to use user-based recommendations. In contrast, if you have fewer items than users, then it is better to use item-based recommendations to gain better performance.

In SVD algorithms, preprocessing can be slow. However, execution is faster than in other methods.

Summary

The Apache Mahout recommendations module helps you to recommend items to users which they have not seen before, based on their previous preferences. The collaborative filtering approach is implemented in Mahout. User-based recommendations, item-based recommendations, and matrix factorization are the key approaches that are geared toward collaborative filtering in Mahout.

Apache Mahout in Production **5**

This chapter talks about achieving scalability in Apache Mahout with an Apache Hadoop ecosystem.

In this chapter, we will cover the following topics:

- Key components of Apache Hadoop
- The life cycle of a Hadoop application
- Setting up Hadoop
    - ○ Local mode
    - ○ The pseudo-distributed mode
    - ○ The fully-distributed mode
- Setting up Apache Mahout with Hadoop
- Monitoring Hadoop
- Troubleshooting Hadoop
- Optimization tips

Introduction

So far, we have discussed key machine learning techniques, such as clustering, classification, and recommendations. However, there are several machine learning libraries, such as MATLAB, R, and Weka out there to implement the preceding techniques.

The volume of available information is growing at an alarming rate. Most of the time, analyzing enormous datasets causes processors to run out of memory. Hence, processing large datasets or datasets with an exponential growth potential is a key challenge in modern machine learning applications.

The key characteristic that makes Apache Mahout shine out from other machine learning libraries is its ability to scale.

In this chapter, you will see how Apache Mahout achieves scalability in a production environment with Apache Hadoop.

Apache Mahout with Hadoop

Apache Mahout uses Apache Hadoop, which is a distributed computing framework, to achieve scalability. The following figure clearly shows the place where Apache Hadoop fits into Apache Mahout:

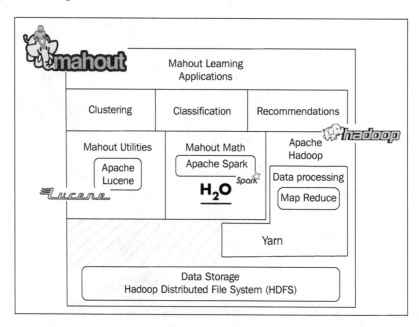

As shown in the previous figure, **Yarn (Data processing)** and **HDFS (Data Storage)** are key components in Apache Hadoop.

In this chapter, we will explain the important subcomponents of **Yet Another Resource Negotiator (YARN)** and HDFS and their behavior in detail before proceeding to the Hadoop installation steps.

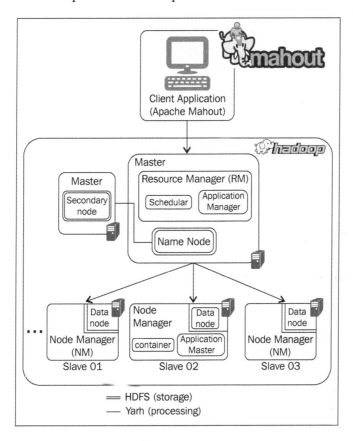

YARN with MapReduce 2.0

First, let's understand YARN, which is a new addition to Apache Hadoop 2.0.

Earlier, Apache Hadoop operated with MapReduce 1.0. It had some drawbacks in cluster resource utilization due to the constraints incurred with the static allocation of map and reduce slots.

YARN, along with MapReduce 2.0, has overcome this drawback by inventing a novel, flexible resource allocation model that contains containers.

The YARN architecture consists of the following subcomponents:

The resource manager

There is one resource manager per cluster to schedule applications (jobs) and manage resource (CPU and memory) allocation globally. The resource manager resides in the master node. The resource manager monitors node managers and application masters by tracking heartbeats. Further, the resource manager ensures the security of the cluster as well.

The application manager

The application manager is responsible for launching application masters in node managers, when an application is submitted for processing. This is a subcomponent of the resource manager.

The resource manager along with the application manager is equivalent to the job tracker in the previous Hadoop version.

A node manager

A node manager is the simplified version of the task tracker in the previous Hadoop version. Resource allocation in the node manager is adjustable, whereas in task trackers, the number of map and reduce slots are fixed.

Node managers reside in the slave nodes of the cluster, and they communicate with the resource manager.

The application master

The application master is the key component that is responsible for gaining better resource utilization in the cluster, and this component does not have a counterpart in the previous Hadoop version.

The application manager executes map and reduce tasks on containers after negotiating for resources with the resource manager. The application master itself is executed in a container, and it monitors and schedules the tasks of a submitted application.

Containers

A particular application submitted for processing can be executed in one or more containers as separate tasks, depending on the resources requested.

Managing storage with HDFS

HDFS is the distributed filesystem that manages data in a Hadoop cluster in a cost-effective and fault-tolerant manner. HDFS has a master-slave architecture. It consists of the following key components:

- **Name node**: The name node plays the role of the master in the HDFS cluster. It manages files and their metadata, such as the number of blocks, rack information for data nodes, and so on.

- **Data node**: The data node is responsible for storing data in HDFS. Also, this is responsible for data replication and HDFS block creation/deletion tasks as well.

- **Secondary node**: The secondary name node is responsible for regularly reading the changes log and applying the changes in the HDFS **fsimage** file, which the name node stores in the HDFS filesystem information.

Now that you have understood the main responsibilities of each component and subcomponent in Apache Hadoop, let's look at the way they interact with each other to get a particular job done.

The life cycle of a Hadoop application

Here, we will explain the life cycle of a machine learning application (for example, a K-Means job) with reference to the following figure:

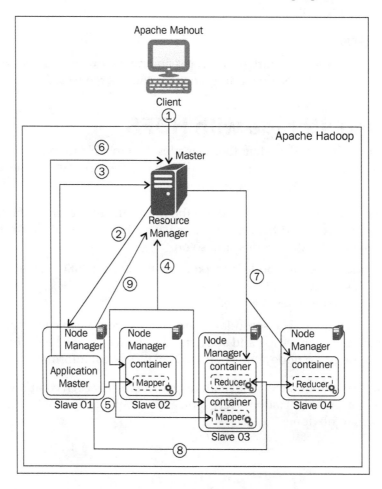

1. The application client (in our case, **Apache Mahout**) submits a new application (job) to the Hadoop **Resource Manager**.

2. The resource manager launches the **Application Master** to manage the submitted application.

3. The **Application Master** requests the required resources (for example, 1 GB memory and 1 core) from the **Resource Manager** in order to execute the map tasks.

4. The **Resource Manager** requests containers that fulfill the resource requirements of the map task in hand from node managers and assigns them to be managed by the application master.

5. The **Application Master** assigns map tasks for the given containers.

6. The **Application Master** requests resources for the reduce task from the **Resource Manager**.

7. The **Resource Manager** assigns containers for the reduce task.

8. The **Application Master** assigns reduce tasks to the assigned containers.

9. Once all the tasks for the submitted application are completed, the application notifies the **Resource Manager** about the completion of the work.

With the preceding information in mind, let's now get our hands dirty with Hadoop installation!

Setting up Hadoop

If you want to run Apache Mahout in local mode (without Hadoop), then you need to set some value for the MAHOUT_LOCAL environment variable, as follows:

```
Set MAHOUT_LOCAL=true
```

Also, if HADOOP_HOME is not set, then Apache Mahout runs locally.

So, if you want to run Apache Mahout with Hadoop, then there are three possible options available:

• Local mode

• The pseudo-distributed mode

• The fully-distributed mode

You can select the Hadoop mode that best suits you, depending on the requirement at hand.

Setting up Mahout in local mode

Local mode is the simplest of all modes in Hadoop with the least number of configuration changes.

Hadoop is running as a single JVM instance in this mode. Hadoop daemons, such as resource manager, name node, node manager, data nodes, and secondary node are not running. Also, there is no HDFS-related file processing with this mode.

Prerequisites

The Hadoop framework is an open source software implementation in Java.

Java installation

Hadoop requires Java 7 or a later version of Java 6. We used Java 1.7.0_76 for this setup.

1. First, copy or download the Java installation.

2. Set the classpath using the following command:

```
export JAVA_HOME=/usr/lib/jvm/java-7-oracle
```

> The instructions to set path variables for Apache Hadoop and Apache Mahout in Ubuntu are given here so that it is easier to execute the commands.
>
> Apache Hadoop:
>
> ```
> export PATH=$PATH:/home/user/hadoop-2.6.0/bin
> ```
>
> Apache Mahout:
>
> ```
> export PATH=$PATH:/home/user/mahout-0.9/bin
> ```

Setting up Mahout in Hadoop distributed mode

Hadoop contains two possible distributed modes:

- Pseudo-distributed mode
- The fully-distributed mode

You can download Apache Hadoop from `https://hadoop.apache.org/releases.html`.

Linux is the supported OS to execute Apache Hadoop operations.

Prerequisites

The following prerequisites are important for both of the previously given distributed modes. So, let's go through them first.

Creating a Hadoop user

A Hadoop user is important in order to communicate with other nodes. Perform the following steps to create a dedicated Hadoop user account:

1. Here, let's create a Hadoop user called `hduser`. You can give any name you prefer, as follows:

   ```
   sudo addgroup hadoop
   sudo adduser --ingroup hadoop hduser
   ```

2. The Hadoop user should have access to the files in the Hadoop installation directory:

   ```
   chown -R huser:hadoop [Hadoop installation directory]/
   ```

Passwordless SSH configuration

In the Hadoop cluster environment, the master node needs to communicate and coordinate with remote slave nodes to execute the submitted applications. SSH is used as a secure communication channel to achieve this aim.

The master node uses public key cryptography (RSA) to communicate with slave nodes. Each slave node has a public key, and the master node uses the private key when communicating.

Perform the following steps to enable passwordless SSH configuration:

1. Switch the current user to the Hadoop user:

   ```
   su - hduser
   ```

2. Generate the SSH key (the RSA key pair with an empty password):

   ```
   ssh-keygen -t rsa -P ""
   ```

3. Enable SSH access to the local machine:

    ```
    .ssh/id_rsa.pub >> $HOME/.ssh/authorized_keys
    ```

4. Verify the SSH connection:

    ```
    ssh localhost
    ```

In the fully-distributed mode, you need to distribute the `ssh` public key among all the slaves.

The pseudo-distributed mode

The pseudo-distributed mode is a simulation of Hadoop clusters in a single server.

If you are a novice in Hadoop, it's always better to play around with pseudo-distributed mode before trying the fully-distributed mode.

All the daemons are run in this mode as separate processes (separate JVM instances) and HDFS is used for storage.

First, copy or download the Hadoop installation and make the Hadoop user the owner of the directory.

Configuration changes

Hadoop configuration changes are located in the Hadoop installation folder, `/etc/hadoop`, for both master and slaves.

There are two types of configuration files in Hadoop, as follows:

*   `*-default.xml`: This reads only default configurations for Hadoop
*   `*-site.xml`: This reads site-specific configurations for Hadoop

You need to do the required configurations in site-specific configuration files.

Refer to the following links for more details on each configuration entry:

*   `Core-default.xml`: https://hadoop.apache.org/docs/stable/hadoop-project-dist/hadoop-common/core-default.xml
*   `hdfs-default.xml`: https://hadoop.apache.org/docs/stable/hadoop-project-dist/hadoop-hdfs/hdfs-default.xml

- mapred-default.xml: https://hadoop.apache.org/docs/stable/
  hadoop-mapreduce-client/hadoop-mapreduce-client-core/mapred-
  default.xml

- yarn-default.xml: https://hadoop.apache.org/docs/stable/hadoop-
  yarn/hadoop-yarn-common/yarn-default.xml

The following code snippet shows the `core-site.xml` file:

```
<configuration>
  <property>
    <name>fs.defaultFS</name>
    <value>hdfs://localhost:9000</value>
  </property>
  <property>
    <name>fs.hdfs.impl</name>
    <value>org.apache.hadoop.hdfs.DistributedFileSystem</value>
    <description>The file system for hdfs: uris. </description>
  </property>
</configuration>
```

The following code snippet shows the `hdfs-site.xml` file:

```
<configuration>
  <property>
    <name>dfs.replication</name>
    <value>1</value>
  </property>
  <property>
    <name>dfs.namenode.name.dir</name>
    <value>file:///home/hduser/hadoop/name</value>
  </property>
  <property>
    <name>dfs.datanode.data.dir</name>
    <value>file:///home/hduser/hadoop/data</value>
  </property>
</configuration>
```

This is how the `mapred-site.xml` file looks:

```
<configuration>
  <property>
    <name>mapreduce.framework.name</name>
    <value>yarn</value>
  </property>
</configuration>
```

The following code snippet shows the `yarn-site.xml` file:

```
<configuration>
  <property>
    <name>yarn.nodemanager.aux-services</name>
    <value>mapreduce_shuffle</value>
  </property>
</configuration>
```

Formatting the DFS filesystem

Before starting the server, you need to format the `namenode` to format the metadata related to DataNodes, as follows:

```
./[Hadoop installation directory]/bin/hdfs namenode -format
```

Starting the servers

Then, start the server using the following commands:

1. Start HDFS by the following command:

   ```
   ./[Hadoop installation directory]/sbin/start-dfs.sh
   ```

   ```
   localhost: starting namenode, logging to /home/hduser/hadoop-2.6.0/logs/hadoop-hduser-namenode-precise32.out
   localhost: starting datanode, logging to /home/hduser/hadoop-2.6.0/logs/hadoop-hduser-datanode-precise32.out
   Starting secondary namenodes [0.0.0.0]
   ```

2. Start YARN (MapReduce):

   ```
   ./[Hadoop installation directory]/sbin/start-yarn.sh
   ```

   ```
   localhost: starting namenode, logging to /home/hduser/hadoop-2.6.0/logs/hadoop-hduser-namenode-precise32.out
   localhost: starting datanode, logging to /home/hduser/hadoop-2.6.0/logs/hadoop-hduser-datanode-precise32.out
   Starting secondary namenodes [0.0.0.0]
   ```

The fully-distributed mode

Hadoop can operate to its full potential in the fully-distributed mode. The master node is in one server, and the slave nodes are in a separate server.

With the master-slave architecture, a large number of servers are working on processing data simultaneously.

In this chapter, we set up the Hadoop cluster with one master and two slave nodes in the Ubuntu environment.

Prerequisites

These are the specific prerequisites to run Hadoop in the fully-distributed mode:

1. Copy the SSH public key for other slave nodes:

   ```
   ssh-copy-id -i $HOME/.ssh/id_rsa.pub hduser@slave01
   ```

2. Enable SSH configuration for all the slaves:

   ```
   ssh-copy-id -i $HOME/.ssh/id_rsa.pub hduser@slave01
   ```

3. Verify the SSH configuration using the following command:

   ```
   ssh master.net
   ```

Host file configuration

Perform the following host file configuration as shown here:

```
etc/hosts - all machines


33.33.33.10     master.net
33.33.33.11     slave01.net
33.33.33.12      slave02.net


33.33.33.10       master


33.33.33.11     slave01


33.33.33.12     slave02
```

```
hduser@master:~$ ssh master.net
Welcome to Ubuntu 12.04 LTS (GNU/Linux 3.2.0-23-generic-pae i686)

 * Documentation:  https://help.ubuntu.com/
New release '14.04.2 LTS' available.
Run 'do-release-upgrade' to upgrade to it.

Welcome to your Vagrant-built virtual machine.
Last login: Tue Mar 17 05:41:29 2015 from 33.33.33.10
hduser@master:~$ 
```

Hadoop configuration changes

The following are the Hadoop configuration changes for the fully-distributed mode:

The `core-site.xml` file:

```
<configuration>
  <property>
    <name>fs.defaultFS</name>
    <value>hdfs://master.net:9000</value>
  </property>
  <property>
    <name>fs.hdfs.impl</name>
    <value>org.apache.hadoop.hdfs.DistributedFileSystem</value>
    <description>The file system for hdfs: uris. </description>
  </property>
</configuration>
```

The `yarn-site.xml` file:

```
<configuration>

<!-- Site specific YARN configuration properties -->

  <property>
    <name>yarn.nodemanager.aux-services</name>
    <value>mapreduce_shuffle</value>
  </property>
  <property>
    <name>yarn.nodemanager.aux-
    services.mapreduce.shuffle.class</name>
    <value>org.apache.hadoop.mapred.ShuffleHandler</value>
  </property>
  <property>
    <name>yarn.resourcemanager.scheduler.address</name>
    <value>master.net:8030</value>
  </property>
  <property>
    <name>yarn.resourcemanager.address</name>
    <value>master.net:8032</value>
  </property>
  <property>
```

```
      <name>yarn.resourcemanager.webapp.address</name>
      <value>master.net:8088</value>
   </property>
   <property>
      <name>yarn.resourcemanager.resource-tracker.address</name>
      <value>master.net:8031</value>
   </property>
   <property>
      <name>yarn.resourcemanager.admin.address</name>
      <value>master.net:8033</value>
   </property>
</configuration>
```

The `hdfs-site.xml` file:

```
<configuration>
   <property>
      <name>dfs.replication</name>
      <value>2</value>
   </property>
   <property>
      <name>dfs.namenode.name.dir</name>
      <value>file:///home/hduser/hadoop/name</value>
   </property>
   <property>
      <name>dfs.datanode.data.dir</name>
      <value>file:///home/hduser/hadoop/data</value>
   </property>
</configuration>
```

Slaves (master only):

```
slave01.net
slave02.net
```

Masters (master only):

```
master.net
```

Formatting the DFS filesystem

Format the HDFS namenode using the following command:

```
./[Hadoop installation directory]/bin/hdfs namenode -format
```

Starting servers

1. Start HDFS using the following command:

    ```
    ./[Hadoop installation directory]/sbin/start-dfs.sh
    ```

```
Starting namenodes on [master.net]
master.net: starting namenode, logging to /home/hduser/hadoop-2.6.0/logs/hadoop-hduser-namenode-master.out
master.net: starting datanode, logging to /home/hduser/hadoop-2.6.0/logs/hadoop-hduser-datanode-master.out
slave01.net: starting datanode, logging to /home/hduser/hadoop-2.6.0/logs/hadoop-hduser-datanode-slave01.out
slave02.net: starting datanode, logging to /home/hduser/hadoop-2.6.0/logs/hadoop-hduser-datanode-slave02.out
Starting secondary namenodes [0.0.0.0]
0.0.0.0: starting secondarynamenode, logging to /home/hduser/hadoop-2.6.0/logs/hadoop-hduser-secondarynamenode-master.out
```

2. Start YARN (MapReduce):

    ```
    ./[Hadoop installation directory]/sbin/start-yarn.sh
    ```

```
starting resourcemanager, logging to /home/hduser/hadoop-2.6.0/logs/yarn-hduser-resourcemanager-precise32.out
localhost: starting nodemanager, logging to /home/hduser/hadoop-2.6.0/logs/yarn-hduser-nodemanager-precise32.out
```

Monitoring Hadoop

Apache Hadoop daemons can be monitored using different mechanisms.

Commands/scripts

The running JVMs related to Hadoop can be displayed using the following command (use the correct Java installation location):

`/usr/lib/jvm/java-7-oracle/bin/jps`

The outcome of the preceding command is given in the following figure:

```
hduser@precise32:~$  /usr/lib/jvm/java-7-oracle/bin/jps
1896 NodeManager
2266 Jps
1488 DataNode
1650 SecondaryNameNode
1790 ResourceManager
1360 NameNode
```

Data nodes

Active data nodes in the cluster can be displayed using the following command:

```
[Hadoop installation directory]/bin/hdfs dfsadmin -report
```

The outcome of the preceding command for a cluster with two data nodes is shown in the following figure:

```
Configured Capacity: 169392562176 (157.76 GB)
Present Capacity: 153689104384 (143.13 GB)
DFS Remaining: 153689047040 (143.13 GB)
DFS Used: 57344 (56 KB)
DFS Used%: 0.00%
Under replicated blocks: 0
Blocks with corrupt replicas: 0
Missing blocks: 0


-------------------------------------------------
Live datanodes (2):

Name: 33.33.33.11:50010 (slave01.net)
Hostname: slave01.net
Decommission Status : Normal
Configured Capacity: 84696281088 (78.88 GB)
DFS Used: 28672 (28 KB)
Non DFS Used: 8657379328 (8.06 GB)
DFS Remaining: 76038873088 (70.82 GB)
DFS Used%: 0.00%
DFS Remaining%: 89.78%
Configured Cache Capacity: 0 (0 B)
Cache Used: 0 (0 B)
Cache Remaining: 0 (0 B)
Cache Used%: 100.00%
Cache Remaining%: 0.00%
Xceivers: 1
Last contact: Thu Mar 19 10:28:38 UTC 2015


Name: 33.33.33.12:50010 (slave02.net)
Hostname: slave02.net
Decommission Status : Normal
Configured Capacity: 84696281088 (78.88 GB)
DFS Used: 28672 (28 KB)
Non DFS Used: 7046078464 (6.56 GB)
DFS Remaining: 77650173952 (72.32 GB)
DFS Used%: 0.00%
DFS Remaining%: 91.68%
Configured Cache Capacity: 0 (0 B)
Cache Used: 0 (0 B)
Cache Remaining: 0 (0 B)
Cache Used%: 100.00%
Cache Remaining%: 0.00%
Xceivers: 1
Last contact: Thu Mar 19 10:28:41 UTC 2015
```

Node managers

Active node managers can be monitored using the following command:

```
[Hadoop installation directory]/bin /yarn node -list
```

The outcome of the preceding command for a cluster with two node managers is shown in the following figure:

Web UIs

Apache Hadoop has provided Web UIs to monitor MapReduce job processing details.

As shown in the following figure, NameNode operations in HDFS can be monitored at `http://localhost:50070/`:

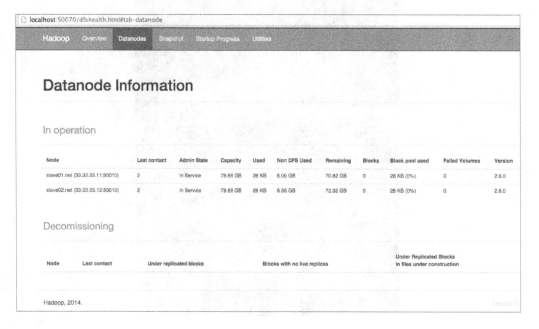

YARN resource manager and node manager operations can be monitored at
`http://localhost:8088/`, as shown in the following figure:

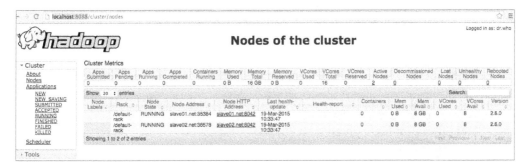

Setting up Mahout with Hadoop's fully-distributed mode

Once Apache Hadoop is successfully installed, we can integrate Apache Mahout
with it using the following simple steps:

1. Download and install Apache Mahout.

2. Set the following environment variables:

   ```
   HADOOP_CONF_DIR="[HADOOP INSTALLATION
   DIRECTORY]/etc/hadoop"

   HADOOP_HOME="[HADOOP INSTALLATION DIRECTORY]"

   MAHOUT_HOME="[MAHOUT INSTALLATION DIRECTORY]"
   ```

Troubleshooting Hadoop

During the installation process, you might encounter issues related to configuration
values, ports, and connectivity problems. Even though it is not possible to provide
solutions for each and every potential issue that you might encounter, the following
hints will be helpful to troubleshoot effectively and efficiently:

1. Check the following environment variable values for different logs:

   ```
   MAHOUT_LOG_DIR

   MAHOUT_LOGFILE
   ```

2. Check the log files at the following location for Hadoop application specific issues:

    ```
    [Hadoop installation directory]/logs/user logs
    ```

3. Make sure that hostnames are specified correctly across all the nodes in the cluster:

    ```
    Check the /etc/hosts file for correct IP/ host name mapping in all
    nodes
    ```

4. Check port numbers for accuracy in the configuration files, and check whether you have given `hostname:port` correctly in all the relevant configuration files.

Optimization tips

Configuring the values of the following configuration entries according to the hardware/software configurations of the Hadoop cluster helps to use the available resources, such as CPU and memory, optimally.

The important configurations in the `mapred-site.xml` file are given as follows:

1. Set the maximum tasks that can be executed in the map phase and the reduce phase:

    ```
    mapreduce.tasktracker.map.tasks.maximum
    mapreduce.tasktracker.reduce.tasks.maximum
    ```

2. Set the number of map and reduce tasks according to number of cores available:

    ```
    mapreduce.job.reduces
    mapreduce.job.maps
    ```

The important configurations in the `hdfs-site.xml` file are given as follows:

1. Set the block size for the files according to the storage requirements of your problem:

    ```
    dfs.blocksize
    ```

However, discussing the performance-tuning approaches for Hadoop in detail is beyond the scope of this book.

Summary

Apache Hadoop plays a key role in Apache Mahout's scalability, which differentiates it from other machine learning libraries.

Apache Hadoop provides data processing (YARN) and data storage (HDFS) capabilities to Apache Mahout. The key components of Apache Hadoop (daemons) are the resource manager, node managers, name node, data nodes, and secondary node.

Apache Hadoop can be installed in three different modes, namely local mode, pseudo-distributed mode, and fully-distributed mode.

Furthermore, Apache Hadoop provides scripts and Web UIs to monitor its daemons.

In next chapter, we will discuss visualization techniques in Apache Mahout.

6
Visualization

In this chapter, we will discuss the visualization techniques for Apache Mahout using D3.js.

This chapter covers the following topics:

- The significance of visualization in machine learning
- D3.js
- A visualization example for K-Means clustering

The significance of visualization in machine learning

"A picture is worth a thousand words"

The ultimate goal of machine learning is to discover better insights from large volumes of data.

If we present the results of a data analysis in table format or as row numbers, it is tiring to perceive the real insights that machine learning has truly obtained. If we visualize the results or the data itself, then it helps us to get a clear picture of the extracted data.

Also, visualization assists us to get the right intuition of the behavior of certain machine learning algorithms easily.

So, visualization is an important aspect in any machine learning application.

However, Apache Mahout does not contain visualization as a component in its library yet.

In this chapter, we will discuss the visualization techniques that can be applied to Apache Mahout using simple integration with D3.js.

D3.js

Data-Driven Documents (D3.js) is a JavaScript library that provides dynamic and interactive data visualizations. It is based on open web standards, such as HTML, CSS, DOM, and **Scalable Vector Graphics (SVG)**.

You can attach your data to DOM elements using D3.js and then you can use HTML, CSS, and SVG to add design properties to the data.

Further, transformations and transitions in D3 provide interactivity with data, which differentiates D3.js from other JavaScript libraries.

A visualization example for K-Means clustering

In this example, we demonstrate the visualization of clusters in K-Means clustering. We use the same example as that given in *Chapter 2, Clustering, K-Means clustering* section (Clustering people based on height and weight).

Follow the given step-by-step guide to come up with a visualization for the previous example using D3.js:

1. Download the D3.js JavaScript file from `https://github.com/mbostock/d3/releases`.

2. You can directly use the web reference as well from `http://d3js.org/d3.v3.min.js`.

3. Create a basic HTML file named `kmeans.html` using any text editor, as follows:

 Save `kmeans.html` in the same directory as the one in which `d3.v3.min.js` resides, or give the path accordingly if you are referencing D3.js as a local resource.

```
<html>
  <head><meta charset="utf-8"></head>
  <body>
  </body>
</html>
```

4. Add D3.js as a reference in the HTML header, as shown here:

```
<head>
  <meta charset="utf-8">
  <script src="d3.v3.min.js" charset="utf-8"></script>
</head>
```

> You can directly give D3.js as a web reference, or you can use the following code:
>
> ```
> <script src="http://d3js.org/d3.v3.min.js"
> charset="utf-
> 8"></script>
> ```

5. You can use any of the web browser inspectors (for example, Firebug) to ensure that D3.js is referenced successfully by typing d3. in the console. You should get a result as shown in the following screenshot:

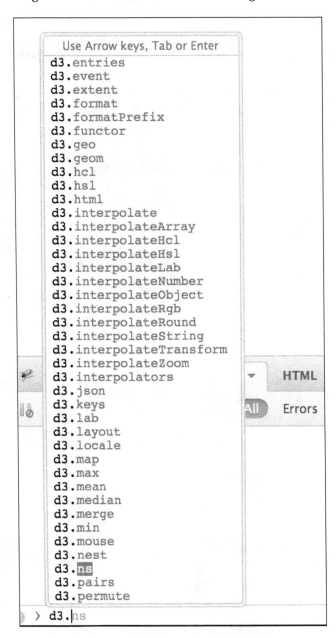

6. Read the data given as the outcome of Apache Mahout. Before proceeding to the D3.js visualization, you need to read the output from the Mahout K-Means clustering algorithm.

    The following screenshot shows the output of the K-Means clustering when read from ClusterDumper:

```
VL-4{n=3 c=[52.667, 149.333] r=[2.055, 3.300]}
      Weight : [props - optional]:  Point:
      1.0 : [distance=2.4267032964268394]: 2 = [55.000, 150.000]
      1.0 : [distance=5.088112507491256]: 2 = [50.000, 145.000]
      1.0 : [distance=3.6817870057290776]: 2 = [53.000, 153.000]
VL-1{n=3 c=[25.000, 80.000] r=[2.449, 4.082]}
      Weight : [props - optional]:  Point:
      1.0 : [distance=3.0]: 2 = [22.000, 80.000]
      1.0 : [distance=5.0]: 2 = [25.000, 75.000]
      1.0 : [distance=5.830951894845301]: 2 = [28.000, 85.000]
```

7. If the K-Means output is directly read from the sequence file, then the output will be as shown in the following figure:

```
key: 3 value: wt: 1.0 distance: 3.0  vec: 2 = [22.000, 80.000]
key: 3 value: wt: 1.0 distance: 5.0  vec: 2 = [25.000, 75.000]
key: 3 value: wt: 1.0 distance: 5.830951894845301  vec: 2 = [28.000, 85.000]
key: 5 value: wt: 1.0 distance: 2.4267032964268394  vec: 2 = [55.000, 150.000]
key: 5 value: wt: 1.0 distance: 5.088112507491256  vec: 2 = [50.000, 145.000]
key: 5 value: wt: 1.0 distance: 3.6817870057290776  vec: 2 = [53.000, 153.000]
```

Either way, you need to extract the data points and centroids from the result in order to use them as input for the D3.js visualization. The method that you can use to achieve this depends on your system architecture.

For example, you can come up with a REST API to send the data from Apache Mahout to D3.js in the JSON format, or you can save the results in the CSV format and read this from D3.js.

The following are the possible options to load data from external resources:

*   A CSV file
*   A tab-Separated Values (TSV) file
*   A text file
*   A JSON blob
*   An HTML document fragment

- An XML document fragment
- XMLHttpRequest (XHR)

In this example, we define an array to hold the data points and centroids, for simplicity. However, please note that it can be replaced with any of the preceding methods:

1. We need to define the data points (x and y), centroids (x and y), and the clusters which the data points belong to, as follows:

```
var dataPoints = [[22.000, 80.000],[25.000, 75.000],[28.000,
85.000],[55.000, 150.000],[50.000, 145.000],[53.000, 153.000]];
var centroids = [[25.000, 80.000],[52.667, 149.333]];
var clusters = [[0],[0],[0],[1],[1],[1]];
```

2. Specify the following constants, which are used during drawing of the clustered points:

```
//X Axis maximum value
var maxX = 100;
// Y Axis maximum value
var maxY = 100;
// Drawing area width
var w =600;
// Drawing area height
var h = 600;
```

3. Use D3.js to add an SVG element to the HTML page using the following statement; the g element is used in SVG to group SVG shapes:

```
var svg = d3.select('#draw').append('svg').attr({'width':w,
'height':h});
var graph = svg.append('g');
```

4. Using the D3.js scale, we convert the numbers in domain to numbers in range. The intention is to move the drawing area toward the center:

```
var xScale =
d3.scale.linear().domain([0,maxX]).range([0,350]);
var yScale =
d3.scale.linear().domain([0,maxY]).range([0,350]);
```

5. The category specifies that we need to construct a new scale with a range of ten colors:

```
var color = d3.scale.category10();
```

Then, data binding is performed for DOM elements using `selectAll` and the `data` elements.

The relevant attributes are set for shapes, such as circles and lines, as required. The X and Y values are determined as given by the data points and centroids arrays.

An example data binding visualization that displays the data points is shown here:

```
var dataPointDots = graph.selectAll('datapoints').data(dataPoints);
dataPointDots.enter().append('circle')
.attr('r', 3)
.attr('cx',function(d){ return xScale(d[0]); })
.attr('cy',function(d){ return yScale(d[1]); });
```

Once you open the `.html` file in your web browser, you will get the following output:

The complete code example for visualizing the K-Means clustering outcome is given as follows, and its outcome can be seen in the following figure:

```html
<html>
  <head>
    <meta charset="utf-8">
    <script src="d3.v3.min.js" charset="utf-8"></script>
  </head>
  <body>
    <div id="draw"></div>
    <script>
      // Outcome from Mahout K-means clustering
      var dataPoints = [[22.000, 80.000],[25.000, 75.000],[28.000,
      85.000],[55.000, 150.000],[50.000, 145.000],[53.000,
      153.000]];
      var centroids = [[25.000, 80.000],[52.667, 149.333]];
      var clusters = [[0],[0],[0],[1],[1],[1]];
      //X Axis maximum value
      var maxX = 100;
      // Y Axis maximum value
      var maxY = 100;
      // Drawing area width
      var w =600;
      // Drawing area height
      var h = 600;

      // Add SVG
      var svg = d3.select('#draw').append('svg').attr({'width':w,
      'height':h});

      // Moving the drawing area towards the center
      var graph = svg.append('g');
      var xScale =
      d3.scale.linear().domain([0,maxX]).range([0,350]);
      var yScale =
      d3.scale.linear().domain([0,maxY]).range([0,350]);
      var color = d3.scale.category10();

      function draw(){
        // Draw data points
        var dataPointDots =
        graph.selectAll('dataPoints').data(dataPoints);
        dataPointDots.enter().append('circle')
        .attr('r', 3)
        .attr('cx',function(d){ return xScale(d[0]); })
```

```
        .attr('cy',function(d){ return yScale(d[1]); });

        // Draw centroids
        var centroidDots =
        graph.selectAll('centroids').data(centroids);
        centroidDots.enter().append('circle')
        .attr('r', 3)
        .attr('stroke', function(d, i) { return color(i); })
        .attr('stroke-width', 3)
        .attr('fill', function(d, i) { return color(i); })
        .attr('cx',function(d){ return xScale(d[0]); })
        .attr('cy',function(d){ return yScale(d[1]); });

        // Draw lines
        var clusterLines =
        graph.selectAll('lines').data(clusters);
        clusterLines.enter().append('line')
        .attr('x1',function(d, i){ return
        xScale(dataPoints[i][0]);
        })
        .attr('y1',function(d, i){ return
        yScale(dataPoints[i][1]);
        })
        .attr('x2',function(d, i){ return xScale(centroids[d][0]);
        })
        .attr('y2',function(d, i){ return yScale(centroids[d][1]);
        })
        .attr('stroke', function(d) { return color(d); });
      }
      // Execute drawing
      draw();
    </script>
  </body>
</html>
```

The resultant output will be as follows:

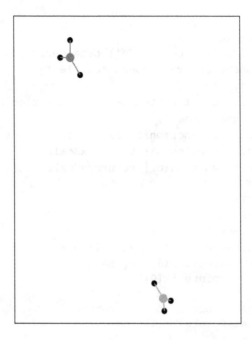

Another prospect of D3.js with the K-Means algorithm is to visualize the way initial randomly-selected centroids and their associated data points iteratively converge into correct clusters in a step-by-step and interactive manner.

This is a great way of understanding the intuition behind developing the K-Means algorithm.

What you have seen is a just a glimpse of what D3.js is capable of doing on top of big data. D3.js can be used to visualize other algorithms, such as linear regression, as well.

However, providing a comprehensive guide on D3.js is beyond the scope of this book.

If you want to learn further, you can refer to `https://github.com/mbostock/d3/wiki/Tutorials` for more information.

Summary

Visualizing data is an important aspect of machine learning. Apache Mahout does not contain an in-built feature for data visualization. However, it can be easily integrated with data visualization tools, such as D3.js. In this chapter, a simple example of visualization was given for Apache Mahout K-Means clustering using D3.js.

Index

N

Naïve Bayes algorithm
  about 66
  Bayes theorem 66
  improvements, by Apache Mahout 68
  Naïve assumption 68
  Markov chain 74
  text classification 66, 67
  text classification coding example 68
Named Entity Recognition (NER) 75
name node 107
Natural Language Processing
      (NLP) tasks 75
nearest neighbour algorithm 93
neighborhood algorithm, user-based
      recommenders 92
  nearest neighbour algorithm 93
  ThresholdUserNeighborhood 93
N-grams 40
node managers
  about 106
  used, for monitoring Hadoop 120

O

Online Gradient Descent 61
OpenCV 6

P

parameters
  convergenceDelta 21
  K 21
  maxIterations 21
  org.apache.hadoop.conf.Configuration 21
  org.apache.hadoop.fs.Path 21
  org.apache.mahout.common.distance.Distance-
      tanceMeasure 21
  runClustering 21
  runSequential 21
Part Of Speech (POS) tagging 75
predictive analytics techniques
  about 48
  model-based prediction 49
  regression-based prediction 48
  tree-based prediction 49

predictor variables 48
pseudo-distributed mode, Hadoop
  about 112
  configuration changes 112, 113
  DFS filesystem, formatting 114
  servers, starting 114

R

real-world example, linear regression with
      Apache Spark
  about 50
  impact of smoking on mortality, and
      diseases 50
Receiver Operating Characteristic (ROC) 66
recommenders 93
reduce function 31
regression
  about 49
  versus classification 49
regression-based prediction
  about 48
  linear regression 48
  logistic regression 48
  Stochastic Gradient Descent (SGD)
      example 48
resource manager 106

S

Scalable Vector Graphics (SVG) 126
secondary node 107
similarity measures
  EuclideanDistanceSimilarity 92
  LogLikelihoodSimilarity 92
  SpearmanCorrelationSimilarity 92
  TanimotoCoefficientSimilarity 92
  UncenteredCosineSimilarity 92
similarity measure, user-based
      recommenders 91, 92
Singular Value Decomposition (SVD)
  usage tips and tricks 100
  using 99, 100
socioeconomic status
  about 51
  URL 51

V

vector space model 39
visualization example, K-Means
    clustering 126-134
visualization, in machine learning
  significance 125, 126
Viterbi evaluator 80, 81

W

Web UIs
  used, for monitoring Hadoop 120, 121
weighted distance measure 28

Y

YARN (Yet Another Resource Negotiator)
  about 105
  subcomponents 106
  with MapReduce 2.0 105, 106

Thank you for buying
Apache Mahout Essentials

About Packt Publishing

Packt, pronounced 'packed', published its first book, *Mastering phpMyAdmin for Effective MySQL Management*, in April 2004, and subsequently continued to specialize in publishing highly focused books on specific technologies and solutions.

Our books and publications share the experiences of your fellow IT professionals in adapting and customizing today's systems, applications, and frameworks. Our solution-based books give you the knowledge and power to customize the software and technologies you're using to get the job done. Packt books are more specific and less general than the IT books you have seen in the past. Our unique business model allows us to bring you more focused information, giving you more of what you need to know, and less of what you don't.

Packt is a modern yet unique publishing company that focuses on producing quality, cutting-edge books for communities of developers, administrators, and newbies alike. For more information, please visit our website at www.packtpub.com.

About Packt Open Source

In 2010, Packt launched two new brands, Packt Open Source and Packt Enterprise, in order to continue its focus on specialization. This book is part of the Packt Open Source brand, home to books published on software built around open source licenses, and offering information to anybody from advanced developers to budding web designers. The Open Source brand also runs Packt's Open Source Royalty Scheme, by which Packt gives a royalty to each open source project about whose software a book is sold.

Writing for Packt

We welcome all inquiries from people who are interested in authoring. Book proposals should be sent to author@packtpub.com. If your book idea is still at an early stage and you would like to discuss it first before writing a formal book proposal, then please contact us; one of our commissioning editors will get in touch with you.

We're not just looking for published authors; if you have strong technical skills but no writing experience, our experienced editors can help you develop a writing career, or simply get some additional reward for your expertise.

Learning Apache Mahout

ISBN: 978-1-78355-521-5   Paperback: 250 pages

Acquire practical skills in Big Data Analytics and explore data science with Apache Mahout

1. Learn to use Apache Mahout for Big Data Analytics.

2. Understand machine learning concepts and algorithms and their implementation in Mahout.

3. A comprehensive guide with numerous code examples and end-to-end case studies on Customer Analytics and Text Analytics.

Learning Apache Mahout Classification

ISBN: 978-1-78355-495-9   Paperback: 130 pages

Build and personalize your own classifiers using Apache Mahout

1. Explore the different types of classification algorithms available in Apache Mahout.

2. Create and evaluate your own ready-to-use classification models using real world datasets.

3. A practical guide to problems faced in classification with concepts explained in an easy-to-understand manner.

Please check **www.PacktPub.com** for information on our titles

Apache Mahout Cookbook

ISBN: 978-1-84951-802-4   Paperback: 250 pages

A fast, fresh, developer-oriented dive into the world of Apache Mahouts

1. Learn how to set up a Mahout development environment.

2. Start testing Mahout in a standalone Hadoop cluster.

3. Learn to find stock market direction using logistic regression.

Getting started with Apache Solr Search Server

ISBN: 978-1-78216-084-7   Duration: 2:30mins

Integrate Solr as a blazing-fast open-source search solution into your enterprise web application and take your application to the next level

1. Teaches you everything you need to know to get started with Apache Solr such as indexing, querying, configuration, and implementation.

2. Learn how to define a search architecture specific to your business needs.

3. Includes walk-throughs on the Solr admin interface.

Please check **www.PacktPub.com** for information on our titles

9781783554997